Enhancing The Educator's Self-Esteem

It's Your Criteria #1!

A Guide for Professional (K-12) Educators

YOU'RE ALWAYS CARING FOR OTHERS,
BUT WHO'S TAKING CARE OF YOU?

For the educator, a healthy self-esteem is job criteria #1. This comprehensive resource for educators defines self-esteem and its importance to our lives and to our work, delineates the ways in which self-esteem is positively or negatively charged in our workplace, and outlines a plan of action for nourishing and enhancing self-esteem in ourselves, our colleagues, and ultimately, the students with whose lives we have been entrusted.

By Bettie B. Youngs, Ph.D.

ʃ

JALMAR PRESS
ROLLING HILLS ESTATES, CALIFORNIA

ENHANCING THE EDUCATOR'S SELF-ESTEEM: It's Your Criteria #1!
A Guide For Professional (K-12) Educators

Library of Congress Cataloging-in-Publication Data

Youngs, Bettie B.
    Enhancing the educator's self-esteem: it's your criteria #1! you're always caring for others, but who's taking care of you? / Bettie B. Youngs
        p. cm.
    Includes bibliographical references
    ISBN 0-915190-79-6 : $16.95
    1. Teachers — United States — Attitudes. 2. Self-Esteem — United States. I. Title.
    LB1775.2.Y68 1992   92-20658
    371.1'001'9 — dc20   CIP

Published by Jalmar Press

ENHANCING THE EDUCATOR'S SELF-ESTEEM:
It's Your Criteria #1!
A Guide for Professional (K-12) Educators

Written by Bettie B. Youngs
Edited by Marie Conte
Production Consultants: Mario A. Artavia II and Jeanne Iler
Cover Design by Jeanne Iler & Mario A. Artavia II
Typography by Mario A. Artavia II
Manufactured in the United States of America
First edition printing: 10 9 8 7 6 5 4 3 2

To Bradley Winch, a most joyous and
esteemed communicator and educator!

A Note From the Author: The terms *he and she* have intentionally been interchanged throughout this text. It is my hope that you will personalize the information in this book for yourself.

Other Works By Bettie B. Youngs, Ph.D.

BOOKS:

Stress in Children (New York: Avon Books, 1985)

Is Your Net-Working? A Complete Guide to Building Contacts and Career Visibility (New York: John Wiley & Sons, 1989)

Friendship Is Forever, Isn't It? (Rolling Hills Estates, CA: Jalmar Press, 1990)

Getting Back Together: Creating a New Relationship With Your Partner & Making It Last (New York: Bob Adams, Inc., 1990)

The 6 Vital Ingredients of Self-Esteem: How to Develop Them in Your Child (New York: Macmillan/Rawson, 1991)

A Stress Management Guide for Young People (Rolling Hills Estates, CA: Jalmar Press, second edition, 1992)

Problem Solving Skills For Children (Rolling Hills Estates, CA: Jalmar Press, second edition, 1992)

Stress Management for Educators (Rolling Hills Estates, CA: Jalmar Press, 1992)

The 6 Vital Ingredients of Self-Esteem: How to Develop Them in Your Students (Rolling Hills Estates, CA: Jalmar Press, 1992)

You & Self-Esteem: It's The Key to Happiness & Success (A Self-Esteem Workbook for Grades 5-12) (Rolling Hills Estates, CA: Jalmar Press, 1992)

A Stress Management Guide for Administrators (Rolling Hills Estates, CA: Jalmar Press, 1993)

Goal Setting Skills for Young Adults (Rolling Hills Estates, CA: Jalmar Press, second edition, 1993)

The Teenager: A Guide to the Adolescent Years (Deerfield Beach, Florida: Health Communications, 1993)

AUDIO CASSETTES:

Helping Your Teenager Deal With Stress (Deerfield Beach, Florida: Health Communications, 1993)

How to Raise Happy, Healthy, Self-Confident Children (Nightengale/Conant, 1990)

The 6 Vital Components of Self-Esteem and How to Develop Them in Your Child (Sybervision, 1990)

Helping Children Manage Anxiety, Pressure, and Stress (Sybervision, 1991)

Developing Responsibility in Children (Sybervision, 1991)

Getting Back Together (Sybervision, 1991)

About the Author

Bettie B. Youngs, Ph. D. is an internationally known lecturer, author, counselor and consultant. Her work has spanned more than 60 countries for more than two decades, earning her a reputation as a respected authority in the field of personal and professional effectiveness. She has earned national acclaim for her work on the effects of stress on health, wellness, and productivity for both adults and children, and for her work on the role of self-esteem as it detracts from or empowers vitality, achievement, and peak performance. Dr. Youngs has conducted extensive research on the stages of growth and development in the K-12 years and their implications for program and curriculum development.

Bettie is a former Teacher-of-the-Year, Professor at San Diego State University, Executive Director of the Phoenix Foundation, and currently serves as a consultant to U.S. schools. She is the author of 14 books published in 23 languages, as well as a number of popular audio cassette programs.

Dr. Youngs, a member of the National Speakers Association, addresses audiences throughout the U.S. and abroad, and meets with nearly 250,000 youth and adults each year. She serves on the Board of Directors for the National Council for Self-Esteem and is a frequent guest on radio and television talk shows. A leader in U.S. education, her consulting firm provides instruction and professional development to school districts nationwide. She may be contacted at:

Bettie B. Youngs & Associates
Instruction & Professional Development, Inc.
3060 Racetrack View Drive
Del Mar, CA 92014
(619) 481-6360

Table of Contents

Enhancing The Educator's Self-Esteem

It's Your Criteria #1!

A Guide for Professional (K-12) Educators

Chapter 1

THE ALL-IMPORTANT SELF-ESTEEM

Self-Esteem Has Far-Reaching Effects

The correlation between self-esteem and one's level of confidence, between self-esteem and achievement, between self-esteem and risk-taking, between self-esteem and goal attainment is well documented. Stanley Coopersmith's historical and ground-breaking research, which gave us a framework for understanding the nature of self-esteem, has made us aware of just how important self-esteem is to our well-being.[1] Other experts, including Nathaniel Branden[2] and Robert Reasoner[3], have pieced together critical elements necessary to its development. Michele Borba[4] connected each element to curriculum content. The National Council for Self-Esteem, a clearinghouse in this field of inquiry, hails self-esteem as a social vaccine, as a panacea in developing personal and social responsibility. It's no secret that self-esteem is somehow factored into the equation that determines the overall quality of one's life. Perhaps nothing affects health and energy, peace of mind, the goals we set and achieve, our inner happiness, the quality of our relationships, our competence, performance and productivity, quite so much as the health of our self-esteem. Because self-esteem is important, we need to know how to care for and nourish it, how to energize it when it's low, and how to rebuild it when it has been eroded.

SELF-ESTEEM. We hear so much about it, but what is *self-esteem*? What detracts from or empowers it? How is it enhanced or eroded in the schoolplace, by the nature of our work, or by those with whom we work? What specific actions can we take, what language can we use, to best encourage positive self-esteem in ourselves and one another? What is the relationship between self-esteem and teaching effectiveness? How does the possession of a high self-esteem result in encouraging self-esteem in our students and colleagues? How does it spark our desire to set and achieve goals? What is its contribution to our enacting a sense of responsibility for ourselves, and on a larger scale, societal or global consciousness, or spiritual enlightenment? Why does a positive self-esteem engender inner happiness and contribute to our attracting healthy and mutually fulfilling relationships? How does the acquisition of a positive self-esteem help us to live up to our full potential, or become "fully functioning persons" as Carl Rogers would say, or become what Abraham Maslow,

Self-esteem is somehow factored into the equation that determines the overall quality of one's life.

---

[1] Stanley Coopersmith. *The Antecedents of Self-Esteem*. San Francisco, CA: W. H. Freeman, 1967.

[2] Nathaniel Branden. *Psychology of Self-Esteem*. Los Angeles: Bantam Books, Nash Publishing Co., 1969.

[3] Robert Reasoner, and R. Gilbert. *Building Self-Esteem: Implementation Project Summary*. ERIC Clearinghouse on Counseling and Personnel Services #CG 029089, 1988.

[4] Michele Borba. *Esteem Builders*. Rolling Hills Estates, CA: Jalmar Press, 1989.

the famous psychologist from Brandeis University, called the "self-actualizing person" and "the fully human person"? Educators recognize self-esteem as central to a student's learning and school success, but what about for us — what is its contribution to the educator's personal and professional effectiveness?

Those are big questions, and important ones. Looking to our self-esteem as a key to finding answers to those questions is an appropriate course of action. There's no doubt about the prominence of its role: Self-esteem is central to how we live our lives in the present, and is at the heart of what we will achieve in the course of our lifetime.

Self-esteem is at the heart of what we will achieve in the course of our lifetime.

Caring for our self-esteem is one of the most important things we educators can do. Because we understand the importance of a positive sense of self for our students, we constantly work to build self-esteem in children, but it's important that we nurture our own self-esteem as well. We too need a base of confidence, positive energy, inspiration, courage, drive, and strength of character in order to sustain high levels of top-notch competence. *The possession of high self-esteem is a prerequisite to being effective in our work.* Just as a student with a positive sense of self is better able to take on the challenge and rigors associated with learning, so the educator with a positive sense of self is better able to take on the extraordinary challenges associated with teaching and working with youth — and in doing so, bring confidence, know-how, high energy, a "can do" competence and performance to the role — over and over again each day, even in the face of daily obstacles. As a result, the educator is more likely to find teaching purposeful and rewarding.

Self-esteem is really that potent.

Self-Esteem — A Definition

Self-esteem is self-regard. It's the value you assign to your personhood. Self-esteem is a composite picture of *self-value.* It's a self-picture — a "total score," your value — your price tag, so to speak. You don't just wake up one morning with negative self-esteem or positive self-esteem, or with a high self-esteem or a low self-esteem. Self-esteem is developed over time. You *earn* your self-esteem.

Author and psychologist Nathaniel Branden, perhaps the father of modern self-esteem philosophy, explains that self-esteem is the intergrated sum of self-efficacy and self-respect.[1] **Self-efficacy** is defined as having confidence in your ability to think, judge, choose, and decide. It's knowing and understanding your interests and needs. It incorporates self-trust and self-reliance. The experience of self-efficacy generates a sense of control over your life, a sense of being at the vital center of your existence — not just a passive spectator and a victim of events. **Self-respect** is defined as having confidence in your values. It's an affirmative attitude toward the right to live and be happy, and to have the freedom to assert your thoughts, wants, needs, and joys. Self-respect allows for mutual regard of others and makes possible a non-neurotic sense of fellowship.

Self-efficacy and self-respect are the dual pillars of healthy self-esteem. If either one is absent, self-esteem is impaired.

Branden explains it this way: "Consider that if an individual felt inadequate to face the challenges of life, if an individual lacked fundamental self-trust, confidence in his or her mind, we would recognize the presence of a self-esteem deficiency, no matter what other assets he or she possessed. Or if an individual lacked a basic sense of self-respect, felt unworthy, or undeserving of the love or respect of others, unentitled to happiness, fearful of asserting thoughts, wants, or needs — again we would recognize a self-esteem deficiency, no matter what other positive attributes he or she exhibited."

High self-esteem is achieved by actively participating in your life in a meaningful way: You refuse to be in an adversarial relationship with yourself, opting instead to be your own best friend. You respect yourself and stand up for yourself in all encounters. You take responsibility for the choices you make, the actions you take, and your behavior — the ways *you* decide to respond to the people and events in your life. You work toward those things that are important to you. You have thought about your values, and your actions are consistent with those values. You actively work to change those things that aren't working well for you — and are willing to self-correct when you recognize you are off course. You want to live your life actively and fully, as opposed to being a bystander or victim. You have thought about what you want, about *how you want to experience your life*, and you have developed plans and intentions for achieving this.

Self-esteem, then, is a consequence.

The Six Facets of Self-Esteem

Coopersmith's historical and ground-breaking research gave us a framework for understanding the importance of self-esteem, and Reasoner's work added belonging and purpose as critical elements to self-esteem development. Other experts including Nathaniel Branden and The National Council for Self-Esteem champion its important contribution to developing personal and social responsibilty. Building on these foundations, my work has led me to believe that there are six key areas in which self-esteem is empowered or eroded. Depending on how positive (esteem building) or negative (esteem eroding) those experiences are, self-esteem is either strengthened or diminished. Positive experiences in these six areas serve to build a positive sense of self, while negative experiences in one or more of these areas seriously erode self-esteem. The overall health of your self-esteem can render you psychologically hardy or vulnerable, capable or incapable, vivacious or despondent. The six vital ingredients of self-esteem are:

Physical safety: Freedom from physical harm.
Emotional security: The absence of intimidations and fears.
Identity: The "Who am I?" question.
Affiliation: A sense of belonging.
Competence: How capable one feels.
Mission: The feeling that one's life has meaning and direction.

ALL Individuals Need a Positive Sense of Self-Worth

All people need to feel a positive sense of self-worth. When there is a feeling of uselessness or despondency about one's life — or when a person feels that he is squandering his time — at first there is anger, then sadness, and soon, despair. *Low self-esteem is registered.* The esteem one holds for one's value is lessened. That's why when educators feel they are making a difference, teaching can be very emotionally rewarding and fulfilling, or desperately trying and unrewarding when they don't. Students have the same need — they need to feel they matter *to us.* Unless a student senses this, teaching is most difficult and retention rate is lowered. Basically, *students don't care how much you know, until they know how much you care.*

Educators especially *need* to feel that they make a difference. At the very core of a great educator is a deep desire to help and lead others — to serve. They need to *know* that they are giving their time — the substance of their lives — to something very special. When an educator feels he or she can no longer meet the needs of students, he or she will work to change this situation, or leave the profession altogether.

> The overall health of your self-esteem can render you psychologically hardy or vulnerable.

Low Self-Esteem Is a Red Flag: It's Time for Human Repair

Perhaps you've noticed that there seem to be a great many more young people (and adults) with special needs today. "At risk" is a common expression used by schools, social service agencies, and the criminal justice system to denote potential risk factors in those young people most likely to fall prey to destructive activities. Once, or so it seemed, only certain students were at risk for becoming involved in destructive behaviors. Not so today. When we aren't paying attention to the emotional life or physical whereabouts of children, then all children are at risk. The increase of destructive behaviors isn't just happening to those students with labels — to economically deprived children, or to those students with parents who are emotionally or physically negligent. Many students are at risk these days. The attendant symptoms — drug involvement, youth pregnancy, dropping out of school, disrespect for educators, parents, and fellow students, apathy, boredom, and other such maladies — show us just how much destruction young people can inflict on themselves and others.

With an increased focus on academics *in the absence of* attention to the important character-building principles that enrich and nourish the inner lives of students, we are likely to see this trend continue. Working with emotionally hungry youths on a daily basis can wear down and take a toll on the esteem of educators. Furthermore, we must deal with the strain of knowing that we cannot help every student with every problem; some difficulties, such as lack of parental care or physical illness or economic shortcomings, are outside of our control. This can cause feelings of helplessness, powerlessness, ineffectiveness — and lessen our sense of competency.

> The very nature of teaching requires an educator with a high level of self-esteem.

The very nature of teaching — being challenged by some thirty to one hundred energetic and not always willing learners each day — requires an educator with a high level of self-esteem.

Students aren't the only ones who can drain our self-esteem, who make demands on us. Our colleagues can often be cynical, demanding, and overly critical of themselves, their students, and us as well. Working side by side with a negative teacher who has low self-esteem puts just that much more of a strain on our own resources, making it even more essential that we maintain high self-esteem in ourselves in order to help others.

Educators Touch Lives and Determine Futures

Educators are *powerful* people not only because we influence the lives of young people daily, but also because what we do and say (and how we do and say it) *becomes the foundation for what youth will make of their lives in the future.* We educators shape the lives of children: We make a difference on a daily basis, even though we may not always be aware of it.

Not all children lead the kind of lives outside of school that you and I might choose for them. For some students, the positive environment in the schoolplace and the emotional health of the teacher are the most positive influences in their lives. Many children find solace in the school because, for them, it's where they can feel a sense of worth. Educators *encourage, show acceptance, instruct, entertain, point out successes,* and *believe* in children. Good educators even *help children believe in themselves.*

We *can* make a powerful difference in our students' lives. If we believe that learning is about empowering our students to stretch the boundaries of their own potential, then we serve youth well. Indeed, one of our prime responsibilities as teachers is to develop potential. We need to understand the relationship of self-esteem to the fulfillment of potential in order to accomplish our goal — to help youth embark on a life that is healthy, functional, and purposeful.

Developing someone else's potential is, as students say, an "awesome" responsibility. Inherent in the role of an educator is a position of leadership, of empowerment. We do this by helping students believe in themselves. In a very real sense, "self perception" is the legacy we give to our students. We help them experience their essence and assign it purposeful value; we help youth feel they matter. This is important because whatever they come to believe, they live out.

Helping students believe that they possess the ability to discover and uncover their own potential, and that they can develop this potential by testing its boundaries, is pretty empowering. To do this, educators themselves must possess high self-esteem. We must care for and enrich our own self-esteem so that we can stay dynamic, enthusiastic, and emotionally healthy.

"Self-perception" is the legacy we give to our students.

A Positive Self-Esteem: Job Criterion #1

Teaching is both exhausting and exhilarating. It's a big-time responsibility, and hard work — much more so than even a decade ago. Today's students *need so much*! A Colorado superintendent best summed it up when he said to me,

"You know, I have the most dedicated, competent, and professional staff I've ever worked with. Our curriculum is aligned with the state frameworks, our materials are up to par, and we have a number of wonderfully designed special services to meet the needs of youth. But you know, the gap between meeting our goals and meeting the needs of our students is wider than ever. Parents are sending us the wrong kids!"

Are you seeing this too? Are you sensing that the more we know about children and the psychology of childhood, the more we research various effective teaching methodologies, the more we understand about learning styles and modalities, and the more we test motivational theories in closing the ever increasing gap between what we want for our youth and their getting it — the more we are forced to look at the role of self-esteem in teaching and learning outcomes? I suspect that's a good thing. If we're serious about developing healthy, happy, competent, self-actualizing students that become functional people, we have to find the *right* formula in order to bring about the *best* results.

Self-esteem is the key. Caring for and enhancing your own self-esteem is an important part of the equation. When you continue to evolve in your own growth and development, the quality, richness, and vitality of your own life adds to that of your students. We can only give and teach that which we are.

DISCUSSION: A Lesson Plan for Educators

1. What is self-esteem? Are the elements that comprise it different in adults and children? Do we all have the same essential factors in self-esteem, or do they vary according to age, race, socioeconomic background, and other factors? How can we define the elements of self-esteem for our students?

2. How does a teacher's self-esteem affect the way he treats his students and fellow teachers? Can we as educators work with our colleagues to help them develop higher self-esteem? Should self-esteem enrichment be part of teacher-training programs?

3. How can a busy educator make self-esteem enhancement a part of the curriculum, especially in content areas such as science and math? Is it possible to have an organized "lesson plan" for self-esteem? How can self-esteem be made a daily part of the teacher's consciousness?

4. What can we as educators do within our own setting to enhance self-esteem in ourselves and our colleagues?

Chapter 2

THE SIX FACETS OF SELF-ESTEEM

Your Self-Esteem Is Showing

Self-esteem is a composite picture of specific and key ingredients that determine how secure, complete, and whole you feel about yourself — your worth. The degree or level of your self-worth is often reflected in your actions. Because actions are motivated by an inner sense of self, others, too, can easily discern the picture you hold of yourself. You wear your self-esteem: It shows! Your actions reflect the reputation you hold with yourself: It's evidenced in your choice of vocabulary, your style of communicating, and the value you assign to others (as can be seen by your treatment of them). Since behavior is a result of your feelings of worth and value, it's a telltale sign of how you feel about yourself.

Your actions reflect the reputation you hold with yourself.

Do You Park Beside Jalopies?

Just as positive self-regard is life expansive, low self-esteem impairs our ability to function in healthy and appropriate ways. Have you ever pulled into a parking space, took note of the car you parked beside, and immediately made a judgment as to whether to stay there or look around for a different space? Perhaps, even though you were parked very close to the car, you decided that the driver would take precautions so as not to ding your car. Or, maybe you moved over so that when the driver of that car opened his door, it wouldn't come into contact with your car.

In either case, the principle that governed your actions — the why you did what you did — was based on the notion that the driver would treat your car as he did his own. If his car appeared unkempt, you instinctively knew that it was unlikely he would be cautious with your car. If he appeared to be careful with his possession, you deduced he would be so with yours, too. Our decisions about how people value themselves, and therefore us, are often based on the same concept. Self-esteem works like that, too. How you feel about yourself determines not only how you take care of yourself, but how you greet and treat other people and respond to each of your experiences.

Suppose you are going to a conference next month and need someone to take over your class. As you think back over the subs you've met this year in deciding whom to ask for, you remember Jan Michaels. She had a firm handshake, was well-groomed, friendly and outgoing. In the few minutes you spent with her, she told you of her children, praising their accomplishments, commented on how much she enjoyed her last teaching assignment, and explained why she is now teaching only part-time. You don't remember the second substitute teacher's name, but you do recall that he wasn't very particular about his appearance and wanted to get right to the specifics on how to discipline those students who didn't "mind" him. Who are you likely to ask for? The first teacher. Why? Because you can tell she thinks well of herself and enjoys her life; she seems in charge of it. Her confidence shows in her security that she can handle the class and make it a good experience for your students as well. Though she wants to know how you want things done, she feels competent to do them in her own professional way. You can tell that she expects to enjoy your class, and therefore, she will.

The degree to which you take responsibility for yourself and your actions is dependent upon the health of your self-esteem. It's unlikely that you've developed a sense of social responsibility if you don't value and respect yourself (personal responsibility). You can't blame your parents, your partner, your faculty or staff members, the administrator(s), or the tough teaching assignment you have for your sense of self. You are responsible for how you care for yourself, and the esteem you ask others to bestow upon you.

The Six Facets of Self-Esteem

There are six elements that empower or erode our sense of self. We can readily see the effects of these elements at work:

■ **A Sense of Physical Safety:** Feeling physically safe means that you aren't fearful of being harmed or hurt. You also care for your health, recognizing it as central to your overall well-being.

■ **A Sense of Emotional Security:** When you know you won't be put down or made to feel less worthy, or be "beat up" emotionally with sarcasm or hurtful words (including the inner messages you send to yourself!), and when you feel that you can confront and deal with your insecurities and fears, you feel emotionally secure. You feel safe in sharing your opinions and ideas. You are respectful and considerate, outgoing and friendly, and caring and compassionate with yourself and others.

■ **A Sense of Identity:** Self-knowledge allows you to develop a realistic sense of self and a healthy sense of individuality. You're friends with the face in the mirror and believe in your worth as a human being. You know yourself, your values, needs, and wants; you are willing to have a friendly, rather than an adversarial, relationship with yourself.

■ **A Sense of Belonging:** When you feel acceptance, you feel a sense of connection to others. Feeling appreciated and valued, you respect, cooperate, and show acceptance of others. You seek to make and sustain friendships. While maintaining a sense of independence, you practice *inter*dependence—a healthy perception of interrelatedness.

You are responsible for the esteem you ask others to bestow upon you.

■ **A Sense of Competence:** Aware of your strengths, you're able to accept the areas where you are less capable, and can do so without developing "victim" behavior. Because you feel capable, you're willing to persevere rather than give up when things become difficult. Because you take initiative, you get results — successes encourage you to try other things. You are empowered through realistic and achievable goals. You take responsibility for your actions.

■ **A Sense of Purpose:** A sense of mission contributes to feeling purposeful. Life has meaning and direction. You set and achieve goals that you deem important. When you encounter obstacles, you generate alternatives that allow you to continue on your way. You have an intuitive nature; you radiate inner knowledge. You are joyful. Your work is more than a job; it's a vocation. You're more likely to agree with the Helice Bridges poster, "I'm not just here to make a living; I'm here to make a difference."

When your experiences in these areas are met in a satisfying and healthy way, what emerges is an enriched capacity to see yourself in command of your actions, capable and competent, loving and lovable, responsible and caring. You have "high self-esteem." Far from being conceited or self-centered, a healthy self-esteem gives you a realistic awareness of yourself, and of your abilities and needs. With an all-encompassing respect for yourself, you are unwilling to allow others to devalue your worth (you are not "just a teacher"), nor will you let them deprive you of your needs. You don't squander your talents and aptitudes, be it through procrastination, substance use, or other means. That you care about your well-being is evident.

> You are empowered through realistic and achievable goals.

Characteristics of High Self-Esteem Teachers

Self-esteem is empowering. What separates the high self-esteem educator from the low self-esteem educator is an attitude of gusto that radiates through one's work. The value of high self-esteem is evident.

■ The higher your self-esteem, the more psychological hardiness you have when coping with adversity and diversity.

■ The higher your self-esteem, the greater zest, zeal, and gusto you bring to the treatment of experiences in your life.

■ The higher your self-esteem, the better able you are to develop and sustain nourishing relationships.

■ The higher your self-esteem, the better able you are to attract others who enjoy their lives and are working to their potentials. Individuals with low self-esteem tend to seek low self-esteem peers who also think poorly of themselves.

■ The higher your self-esteem, the better able you are to feel satisfaction from your accomplishments.

■ The higher your self-esteem, the better able you are to find ways to get along well with others and respond positively to them. You strive to be useful, helpful, purposeful, and responsive.

■ The higher your self-esteem, the better able you are to exercise compassion for yourself and others. Compassion exposes self-worth: It is a sign that you have *discovered the treasured **value** of your personhood.*

■ The higher your self-esteem, the more secure, decisive, optimistic, and purposeful you are or, as we say, "empowered."

High self-esteem individuals focus on the positive experiences.

■ The higher your self-esteem, the better able you are to recognize your own worth and achievements without a constant need for approval from the outside. This does not mean that you don't need others, but rather, that you are interdependent (vs. dependent) with them.

■ The higher your self-esteem, the more responsibility you take for your actions, the more accountable you are. Personal responsibility is the entree to social responsibility.

■ The higher your self-esteem, the more willing you are to accept challenges, to *extend your boundaries* because you have experienced previous successes.

Recognition of personal strengths and capabilities serves as a powerful coping and buffer strategy for overcoming obstacles, and helps compensate for weaknesses and setbacks. We have all met with our fair share of failure, but high self-esteem individuals focus on the positive experiences; they draw their strength from these rather than from the negative and energy-draining encounters.

DISCUSSION: A Lesson Plan for Educators

1. How does your own self-esteem show? Give examples of your appearance, actions, thoughts, moods, and other facets of your life that are reflections of high or low self-esteem. Can a person with low self-esteem hide his feelings about himself?

2. How are students impacted by an educator's high or low self-esteem? Give specific examples of teachers you know who have had a positive or negative effect on their students? Show how the effects of negative self-esteem can be turned around so as to help, rather than hinder, students.

3. Can educators (or students) be involved in raising an educator's sense of self-esteem? Are other educators (or students) aware of the teacher's sense of self?

4. How can educators enhance self-esteem (their own) in the workplace?

TESTING FOR SELF-ESTEEM: YOURS

Assessing Self-Esteem

With self-esteem being so central to your well-being and to positive outcomes in your work, how can you determine whether or not your self-esteem is a healthy one, or in need of repair? The following guidelines can give you some indication. Ask yourself:

Indications of High Self-Esteem

■ **Do I Actively Participate?** Educators with high self-esteem are willing, even eager, to participate, to get involved. When invited to join in a special school-related activity or function, do you look forward to the fun of being together with peers and to participating in the activity at hand? When asked to join a particular group, or participate in a project or a discussion at a faculty meeting, do you do so willingly? In an in-service educational program, do you eagerly look forward to learning a new idea or concept, or are you often reluctant? For example, do you sit there correcting papers, knitting, or chatting in the back row with friends? Do you sit in the meeting with your arms folded high across your chest? Educators with a healthy self-esteem are likely to participate joyfully in a number and range of experiences. They have a curiosity, a desire to experiment, a natural willingness to try out new ways of being effective, and a friendliness about being with others. *How about you*? How do *you* respond?

Do you eagerly look forward to learning a new idea or concept?

■ **Do I encourage and compliment others?** Educators with high self-esteem encourage others and cheer them on. Able to accept praise and receive compliments themselves, they are willing to compliment and praise others in return. They are the first to say, "Your students are so fond of you! They really think you're great!" or "Hey, that class project you tried with your students really worked. Those kids are still talking about it. I'd love to hear more about what you did that made it such a great learning experience for them." Low self-esteem teachers, on the other hand, won't risk building you up; they are unable to give themselves or others positive and encouraging language. Are you able to encourage and compliment others? Do you?

■ **Do I accept advice without viewing it as criticism?** Educators with high self-esteem are able to take constructive feedback with an attitude of acceptance.

In fact, they actively solicit feedback. Performance reviews, team teaching, and classroom visitations by other educators are not viewed as intimidating, but rather with a "How am I doing? What could I do differently that would be beneficial for my students?" kind of attitude. They are secure and willing to accept guidance and direction because they want to be effective. Low self-esteem teachers, on the other hand, view advice as criticism or as a form of rejection. Fearful of how others will view them, they seldom talk about teaching methods, student outcomes, or new curriculum ideas. Instead, their chatter is aimed at criticizing reluctant learners and low self-esteem students, or taking pot shots at the students' parents.

■ **Do I think of my peers as a team?** Educators with healthy self-esteem think of the total faculty and staff as a team; they approach their work with a synergistic attitude. Do you only associate with one particular group, or are you a part of an isolated clique? Or do you make an effort to mingle and talk with all staff members because you recognize that serving the students requires that the entire staff work together? Do you know your district's mission, do you possess a copy of the formal mission statement(s)? Are you familiar with your school's philosophy? Do you discuss this philosophy with your colleagues?

■ **Am I a great teacher?** Educators with a healthy self-esteem *want* to be effective. You want your students to learn and achieve, so you aren't intimidated by tackling the challenge of understanding a new way to teach, of examining and trying out a new curriculum, nor do you stop searching for ways to reach out to the reluctant or the low self-esteem learner. Would you describe yourself as a great teacher? Are you an active and willing learner?

■ **Am I relationship oriented**? Educators with a healthy self-esteem are genuinely caring. They want to know students and fellow educators as individuals; they make a point of talking with students and of getting to know their colleagues as individuals. Do you? Do you share conversations about life outside the realm of teaching with your colleagues?

■ **Do I think globally, act locally**? Educators with high self-esteem are conscious of their leadership role and are active in their communities. In turn, they seek to develop in their students a desire to be responsive to their community and, on a larger scale, world conditions. These educators know that the road to world peace is achieved person-by-person. They know that by acting locally, they affect globally — by instilling purposeful values of peace, caring and sharing within their students, they truly make a difference in the world.

■ **Have I developed interests outside of the school?** Educators with high self-esteem recognize that the schoolplace is just one facet of their lives. While you draw a great deal of satisfaction from your work, do you enrich your life with other activities as well? Do you spend time with family and friends, participate in sports or hobbies, or get involved in your community?

■ **Am I taking responsibility for myself and my actions?** With a high self-esteem, you are more likely to take responsibility for your life and feel a sense of control over it.

> Educators
> with high
> self-esteem
> are conscious
> of their
> leadership role.

Indications of Low Self-Esteem

The signs indicating low self-esteem may take diametrically opposite forms, manifesting themselves in emotional withdrawal or showing up in a passive-aggressive relationship with fellow colleagues. Those with low self-esteem may insist on maintaining the status quo, resist new challenges (such as trying a new curriculum), or refuse to embrace ideologies necessary to student learning (for example, the philosophy that "all students can learn"). Here are a few of the more general signs that signal a low sense of self-esteem.

■ **Constant self-belittling.** Educators who are always remarking, "I can't," or "I'm not," or "I'm just a teacher," or other self-defeating remarks that contribute to their feeling unworthy, have low opinions of themselves. While we all make comments of this sort on occasion, it's time for concern when these self put-downs become a frequent part of our communications.

■ **Refusal to be the best they can be**. If an educator never makes an attempt to "strive toward excellence" (or to take the initiative to live up to his own standards of an effective educator), it might be because the educator feels he can never be as good as other teachers are and lacks the self-confidence and self-esteem to risk those behaviors necessary in making a change. When you simply don't care about being the best you can be, and are unwilling to self-correct, you're exhibiting low self-regard.

■ **Excessive criticism of others.** When an educator constantly criticizes you, his students and/or their parents, the administration and others, it indicates he has a lack of confidence in himself and feels that in order to build himself up, he must belittle those around him. This is his way (though he may not be conscious of it) of trying to feel superior, to escape from his feelings of inferiority.

While you can't always control what happens to you, you can control your reactions.

■ **Excessive concern with the attention and opinions of peers.** Educators who give too much importance to the attention and opinions of friends are rarely able to assert their judgment when faced with the disapproval of their peers, because they don't trust their thinking. They endorse the values and actions of others, even when they know those actions are contrary to what they really believe.

How Your Day-to-Day Activities Affect Self-Esteem

The following exercise can help you examine your specific day-to-day activities to see how certain events (some within your control, some wholly outside of it) can affect your self-esteem. While you can't always control what happens to you, you can control your reactions, thereby monitoring an event so as not to let it lessen your self-esteem. The goal is to examine how the events of your day add to or detract from your positive sense of self, and how events are less important than your response to them. *How you respond* affects your sense of self. The good news is that your response is in *your* control.

To begin, briefly write out the events of any given day — it could be the events of yesterday, today, or something that happened last week. I've provided an example scenario (Elaine's Day) as a way to show you how to depict those events. You'll need to make a copy of the self-esteem charting grid for your own use; my suggestion would be that you duplicate about 20 of these so that you can do this exercise for yourself on a regular basis. I recommend that you do this daily for one month in order to get an overall sense of how day-to-day activities accumulate to enhance or erode your sense of self.

Begin by reading the statements that describe Elaine's day. After each statement put a mark to describe how you think it would affect her self-esteem that day. For example, if the student Elaine thought was least likely to show up with his work done not only shows up early to class but with the class project completed — colored charts and all — she might rate it as a 7, 8, 9, or 10. If, heaven forbid, the district curriculum director makes an unexpected visit to her classroom and she feels frumpy in that purple dress, or unprepared in her lesson, maybe a 2, 3, or 4 would be tallied.

Think about how the little things that happen to you each day affect your *overall* self-esteem.

Some events do not have much of an effect on self-esteem. If she heard that a twelfth grade student was accepted to a prestigious four-year college, she might not be affected one way or the other, since she didn't have the student in class and didn't know him (though if school spirit is high, it might evoke a sense of pride and trigger a more spirited response). The goal of this exercise is to help you think about how the little things that happen to you each day affect your *overall* self-esteem. Again, the best picture would come not so much from doing this exercise for a day, but from doing it over a period of time.

Elaine's Day

Self-Esteem Rating

a. Elaine wakes up to her clock radio playing her favorite song.

b. She decides to wear *that* purple dress. She doesn't like it, but wants to get some use out of it before it finds its way into the Goodwill basket!

c. As Elaine steps out of the shower, she notices the cup of coffee her husband has brought to her with a note attached reading, "Good morning, my sweetheart!"

d. At the breakfast table Elaine's sixteen-year-old daughter, Amy, tells her that Michael, the most popular boy in the school, said he thought her friend, Geena, was cute, but dumb.

e. Amy tells her mom that she looks "rad." When Elaine says, "Thank you, you always say the nicest things to me!" Amy says, "Well, you're a great mom!"

f. During lunch, Elaine notices Coach Lamont Adams staring at her. Elaine and Lamont had an argument the day before about the low grade that made his best athlete ineligible for the football team. Lamont looks right at Elaine then purposely turns his back on her.

g. Elaine's fourth-period class seems quite annoyed with her refusal to put off the chapter final just because the school is having a play that night.

h. A fourth-period student, Roger, shows up to class with his project completed, colored charts and all. Elaine had given him one last chance to complete the project, but was doubtful that he cared enough about his grade and their relationship to do the project — in spite of her *last attempt* to warn him.

i. Elaine gets called over the intercom to come to the counseling office immediately after school. When she arrives, Mr. Roth is angry about his son's grade. Elaine has spent considerable time with Randy Roth and has gone out of her way to help him succeed. Mr. Roth looks at Elaine and says, "You teachers are all the same. You don't care about anybody . . ."

j. As Elaine is reading over papers for her last period class, she notices a little smiling face drawn on the last page with a note from the student reading, "Thanks for giving me extra time! It was helpful and I really appreciated it!"

She notices a little smiling face drawn on the last page.

k. That night her son brings home an English paper with an A+ on it.

l. Elaine's dog, Bart, sensing that Elaine is tired, hops up on her bed and lies next to her, looking sad.

Here's how Elaine ranked these events in terms of their importance to her. How does this ranking compare to the way you thought her perception of self might have been affected by each of these events?

	Low Self-Esteem				No Effect			High Self-Esteem		
	1	2	3	4	5	6	7	8	9	10
Event a								X		
Event b		X								
Event c									X	
Event d					X					
Event e										X
Event f	X									
Event g						X				
Event h									X	
Event i	X									
Event j									X	
Event k										X
Event l								X		

Using the example of Elaine's day as a model, do this exercise for the events in your day. Doing so can help you gain a better understanding of how your experiences contribute to *empowering* or *eroding* your self-esteem. When you're finished rating each one, connect the dots to get an overall image of the effect these events have on your self-esteem.

DESCRIPTION OF YOUR DAY

You can gain a better understanding of how your experiences contribute to *empowering* or *eroding* your self-esteem.

a. _____

b. _____

c. _____

d. _____

e. _____

f. _____

g. _____

h. _____

i. _____

j. _____

	Low Self-Esteem				No Effect			High Self-Esteem		
	1	2	3	4	5	6	7	8	9	10
Event a										
Event b										
Event c										
Event d										
Event e										
Event f										
Event g										
Event h										
Event i										
Event j										

THE SELF-ESTEEM PROFILE FOR EDUCATORS

© 1991 Bettie B. Youngs, Ph.D.

This next assessment can help you understand how specific areas detract from or empower your sense of self by delineating your feelings in each of the six vital areas of self-esteem. Read each of the following statements in the six categories. Think for a moment about each one, and then decide whether the statement for you is true or false. Don't think about each statement too long, or try to analyze it. While your response to the questions may vary from time to time, respond to the questions by thinking about how you feel *most* of the time. Go with your first response.

Physical Safety

T F 1. I'm not afraid of any student (or staff member) at my school.

T F 2. I don't mind being alone in my classroom, or at school before or after hours.

T F 3. I seldom get a headache or have muscle tension at the end of the day.

T F 4. I am physically fit and take excellent care of my health.

T F 5. I am not fearful of walking to and from my car when I arrive or leave my workplace.

Emotional Security

T F 1. Faculty, students, and administrators give me feedback about my being an effective educator.

T F 2. Other educators will listen as I talk about how things are going for me.

T F 3. Our faculty is really close; we care about each other.

T F 4. I give myself credit when I do something well.

T F 5. I try never to make fun of other colleagues or students; I don't tease or name-call unfairly.

I like being an educator.

Selfhood, Identity

T F 1. I like being an educator.

T F 2. I like who I am.

T F 3. I take care with my appearance, trying to look my best every day.

T F 4. I'm proud to tell others that I'm an educator.

T F 5. I have interests outside of my workplace.

Affiliation, Belonging

T   F   1. I like to be with my colleagues.

T   F   2. Whenever I say I'll do something, my students, colleagues, and administrator know I can be counted on.

T   F   3. I like my colleagues and my students, and strive to develop positive relationships with them.

T   F   4. My peers know they can count on me for support and advice.

T   F   5. I like being included in faculty activities at school and in outside social events by staff members.

Competence

Teaching is really purposeful for me.

T   F   1. I set goals and achieve them.

T   F   2. I know a lot about students — especially the age of learner I teach.

T   F   3. I'm a good educator; I feel prepared for the job.

T   F   4. I don't always succeed with every student, but I always give him or her my best.

T   F   5. I rarely encounter a problem I can't handle.

Mission, Purpose

T   F   1. I'm in my chosen career.

T   F   2. Teaching is really purposeful for me.

T   F   3. My life has meaning and direction.

T   F   4. I find value in working with youth.

T   F   5. I am a fulfilled person.

Scoring the Self-Esteem Profile

As you probably guessed, these questions were designed to illicit a True response. Look back over your responses. The best way to get an idea of how the content in each category affects your self-esteem is to look at each category separately. If you had two or more False responses in any single category, this is probably an area in which low self-esteem is causing problems for you. For example, if you had several False answers under "Affiliation, Belonging," examine why that is so. Do you avoid being with your colleagues? Are you truly not included in faculty activities, or do you simply overreact to an unintentional omission? If you feel that your colleagues don't come to you for advice, do you purposely not go to them for advice, even if you need it and they could help you? Once you have identified these areas, the next step is to see how the low self-esteem engendered by these feelings impacts your life and work.

DISCUSSION: A Lesson Plan for Educators

1. Is it fair and reasonable to expect your colleagues to identify weaknesses in your self-esteem and attempt to remedy them? Can someone else truly affect your self-esteem, or is that something only you can do for yourself? Could your school develop a program to help teachers help each other enhance their self-esteem?

2. How can you tell when your self-esteem is low for justified reasons that need changing, or when you are simply being hard on yourself for no good reason? When does low self-esteem indicate a need to take action?

3. Is there ever a time when low self-esteem is normal — say, during a crisis, such as a divorce or being fired from work?

4. When issues are outside of your control, how can you keep from letting them lower your self-esteem? Can others help? How?

Chapter 4

PHYSICAL SAFETY AND WHAT IT MEANS

The First Prerequisite: Physical Safety

How you are faring in each of the six key areas — physical safety, emotional security, identity, belonging, competence, and purposefulness — is central to the state (health) of your self-esteem. Physical safety — the most basic of needs according to Maslow's hierarchy — is the first in the hierarchy of the six ingredients of self-esteem.

Physical safety is central to feeling emotionally secure.

The essence of safety is a sense of moving about the world with freedom — in the absence of fear. Because you are not dominated or coerced, you are in control of your *self* in your environment — you have mastery over your being. An inner feeling of outer safety is a prerequisite for progressing to the other five areas, and thus developing a whole sense of self. Feeling physically safe is so crucial that, without it, the development of a strong and healthy self-esteem is severely limited.

Being physically safe means that you aren't fearful of being hurt in any way, anywhere — in your home, neighborhood, community, or school. You are well, not suffering from a terminal or incurable disease; you are fit, in good health and well. Physical safety is central to feeling emotionally secure.

As a consultant to schools in the United States and abroad, I'm frequently on an airplane. Once aboard, I don't get comfortable, nor do I begin reading, editing, or sharing a conversation with a neighboring passenger until the engines sound hearty and take-off gets behind us. Then, when we're in the air and all feels safe, I relax and become productive. The airlines, too, know that my feelings of physical safety are important. Shortly after passengers board, a flight attendant announces, "Welcome aboard. Your safety is our number one priority. Please give us your attention so that we can tell you about the safety rules designed to . . ."

Just as in the airline industry, physical safety is your school's number one priority, and if you think about it, it's probably your number one concern in the classroom, too. When students feel physically safe in the classroom and in the school environment — when they don't have to worry about being hurt by anyone — they can move on to being learners. They need all their energies to confront the daily schedule of planned activities, to concentrate on learning endeavors, and to achieve and excel scholastically.

Unfortunately, not all schools provide a *safe* environment, and not all students and educators feel safe in the schoolplace: Sadly, student violence escalates every year. Common incidents of such violence include verbal and physical threats, assaults, injury, theft, arson, and vandalism. According to a recent safe school study, the scope of criminal activity in America's schools is alarming. The study reported that in a typical *month,* 282,000 students were physically attacked; 112,000 students were robbed by someone using weapons or threats; 2.4 million students had personal property stolen; 800,000 students stayed home from school because they were afraid to attend; 2,400 fires were set in schools; and 1,000 teachers were assaulted seriously enough to require medical attention. Is it any wonder so many children and more and more teachers are frightened?

An unsafe school environment creates a sick environment. In addition to the obvious seriousness of being a victim of a crime, all students and educators are indirectly and seriously affected by the threat of physical harm (and that includes emotional abuse) in the schoolplace. The toll is more than a physical one. For example, when a child views the school as a hostile environment, he is more likely to dislike the school, teachers, and fellow students. Research shows that youth who are afraid at school are more likely to rate themselves as below-average students, and actually do receive lower grades. Fear reduces a student's ability to concentrate on schoolwork and indicates an atmosphere of mistrust. It undermines morale and indicates that the staff is not in control — that student disorder is more powerful than the adult call for order. Students who have been victims of attack, robbery, or verbal abuse often admit that they are afraid on the way to and from school, and while they are actually in school. If their uneasiness becomes intolerable, they will stay away from school altogether. Currently, more than one million children drop out of school each year, and the figure continues to increase.

Fear reduces a student's ability to concentrate on schoolwork and creates an atmosphere of mistrust.

Not All Teachers Staying at Home Have the Flu!

For the educator, feelings of low self-esteem can result from knowing that we can't always protect children, as much as we would like to ensure that all of them will have a safe and enriching experience while at school. Added to this is the fact that educators may not be so safe there either. Each year more and more teachers leave the profession, citing the jeopardy of their safety as a reason for their exit.

Science teacher Rick Sulisky was the last person anyone would feel was afraid for his physical safety. He was six feet tall, in good physical condition, and considered a good educator by his students and peers. But when some of the larger boys in the class began talking back to him, even to the extent of hovering next to him, he lost his confidence. Though Rick could handle the boys one on one, he felt intimidated when they would gather in groups of five or six and surround him, teasing him about throwing acid from the chemistry lab in his face. "I wake up every morning fearing that class," he said. "I keep telling myself that I'm in control and they're just kids. But it's wearing me down. Once they planted a little seed of fear in me, it just kept growing and growing. Now I look at my students differently and wonder what they are going to do to me rather than what I can do for them. I'm beginning to be fearful, and like teaching less. I feel like I'm not giving my best, that my fear is making me less effective. I'm surprised that a few sixteen-year-olds can make me feel so shaky, but it just seems that students are so much more bold and disrespectful of teachers. It's not like when I went to school."

Rick is a classic example of a teacher whose self-esteem is lowered because of a threat to physical safety (whether real or imagined). The threat to one's personal safety is not confined to fearing others. Arlyn is a 48-year-old elementary school teacher. His third graders love him, and it's obvious he's a devoted educator. Yet lately, he has become a bit sarcastic and cynical. Last month, there were two fires caused by faulty wiring in an old and outdated building in which he teaches. They were very small fires, quickly put out and shrugged off by central administration as something that was bound to happen now and then. But the fires frightened Arlyn. He couldn't stop thinking about them, wondering what he would do if a fire started in his classroom. He began having nightmares about not being able to lead his students out to safety in time. He felt more and more insecure, especially when he realized that the district had made no provisions for repairing or enhancing this dilapidated building. Arlyn's self-esteem plummeted as he lost respect for a career he truly loved.

Feeling Safe At School: Six Protective Measures You Can Take

Some of the rules and procedures put in place to protect students also provide protection for you. Here are some things you can do to safeguard your well-being.

Posted rules help make it clear to each student that you value the safety of everyone in the room.

■ **Alert parents (as well as your students) to classroom rules and procedures.** Protecting your well-being in the schoolplace begins with protecting your students' well-being. The rules you put in place to govern physical safety in the classroom are designed to protect *all* students. Posted rules help make it clear to each student that you value the safety of *everyone* in the room. Be sure that students know these rules and why they are in place, as well as how they will be reinforced, and then be sure that parents understand the same. Ask parents to support classroom safety by encouraging their children to adhere to these rules.

■ **Make sure that parents (as well as your students) are aware of the policies that govern school-wide safety.** Be sure that parents are aware of the rules that exist for safety in the school environment. Again, be sure that each child knows what the rules are, and ask parents to inform their children about the importance of following them.

■ **Learn about school security.** Security procedures are necessary in every school. The best ones are unobtrusive, of course. If rules are lacking or not enforced in your school, arrange a time to meet with the principal and your teacher representation board to discuss what can be done. Measures to ensure physical security must focus on guaranteeing internal control of the school and external control of its perimeter. Take the time to talk to the school principal, grounds-keeper, or security officer about what safety measures are being used on your school campus. Questions include:

- Do teachers regularly walk through corridors and around the grounds?
- Is the cafeteria supervised?
- Are all school-related functions well supervised?
- Does a patrol car come by to check out the parking lot during evening activities?
- Is the campus well lighted at night?

■ **Report students you suspect are carrying weapons.** If you suspect that some students are prone to carrying dangerous objects or weapons, inform the administration and be sure the situation is dealt with. Don't wait for an incident to happen before you do something to protect yourself and others.

■ **Work to bring about school policy that ensures a safe and orderly environment.** Be assertive about the importance of bringing about a safe and orderly environment. Be an advocate. Students and educators feel more secure in classrooms and schools where safety measures are in place. Support those practices that uphold the value of safety. For instance, is the student-teacher ratio manageable — does it lend itself to promoting a safe and orderly environment? Class size and school size *do matter*. If you are having a hard time convincing others, turn to the research that bears out what makes for a good school, effective teaching, and achievement in students. You'll see that the ideal student/teacher ratio for elementary school is about 18 to 24 children per teacher; for middle school about 25 to 28; and for high school, 28 to 32. These ratios are a good practice for all children and educators, most especially in those schools or classrooms where children have special learning and/or emotional needs.

■ **Ask your school to provide parent programs on ways to discipline their children effectively.** Children who have been taught appropriate ways to behave (at home) most likely demonstrate appropriate behavior at school. Unfortunately, with the new family dynamics going on — including more stepfamilies and single-parent working families, parents in emotional chaos and/or in stressful job and career roles, families under increased economic pressures, and children exposed to seeing children on television with the same rights and privileges as adults — today's students seem to respect their teachers and other authoritarian figures less. As a result, more and more children are showing emotional strain, lacking adequate guidance and direction (and self-control), and having more severe behavioral problems. By providing workshops for parents at each grade level, schools can offset some of these harsh realities and their effects on students. Parents find such training both useful and helpful. A good parenting workshop should help parents:

- know how to help their child in the role of a learner

Be assertive about the importance of bringing about a safe and orderly environment.

- learn about their child's stage of growth and development
- understand the dynamics of behavior management
- determine reasonable goals and expectations for their age of child
- teach their children how to be responsible
- learn how to set boundaries for their children's behavior, reinforce positive behavior, and enforce appropriate consequences for inappropriate actions
- examine their parenting philosophy to determine how it compares and contrasts with their parenting partner and what they can do if such differing styles aren't providing a positive model for their children

You can be reassured that there are ways to confront even the most difficult problems.

■ **Study other schools.** If you have become afraid for your own physical safety at school, look at other schools to see what their safety records are like. If some of those schools are old, what special measures do they take to ensure protection from fires, earthquakes, or storms? If the schools are in "bad" neighborhoods, how do they handle security? If the schools have a notorious student body, what special procedures are involved in their day-to-day disciplinary measures? By learning how other schools cope with problems, you can be reassured that there are ways to confront even the most difficult situations. It's not always easy to "solve" or "cure" a problem, but again, your reaction and your sense of power in affecting an outcome determine its effect on your self-esteem. By being aware of the safety problem and taking steps to remedy it, or as the alternative, leaving an environment where your safety is in jeopardy, you'll feel better about yourself.

DISCUSSION: A Lesson Plan for Educators

1. What safety rules have you put in place in your classroom? Are they adequate? Is your list too long? Have you shared this list with parents? Do you periodically review these rules with your students, sharing why these are important and how they are designed to provide protection?

2. How much do you know about the physical plant of your school? Are you aware of any problems, such as faulty wiring or difficult exit doors? What can be done to correct the problems or minimize their negative effects on safety? Do you feel comfortable discussing these problems with your school administration?

3. Is there open communication about physical safety within your school, or is it taken for granted and shelved in favor of discussing more pressing problems, such as budgeting and curriculum revision? How can you ensure that safety is kept a primary topic of discussion?

4. How can you encourage colleagues to talk about their safety fears without fear of being ridiculed or being thought of as foolish?

Chapter 5

PHYSICAL SAFETY: ARE YOU HEALTHY AND FIT?

Would Your *Body* Say You Are Fit?

If you went to work each day to a dilapidated building, a school that had plaster crumbling, paint peeling, and walls sagging, you would feel pretty insecure. If someone asked you where you worked, you might say something derogatory or change the subject. You wouldn't want to admit you worked in such a run-down place. But what about where you live? I don't mean your house, but your body. Your body is your own building, your foundation, the shell that you exist in. You know when you haven't done the maintenance to keep it in shape, and undoubtedly, you are well aware of how that makes you feel.

Priscilla Scoulton, my high school physical education teacher, once said to me, "When your body is fit and healthy you always feel good about yourself." Given how fit and exuberant she was, it made a lot of sense to me at the time. Over the years I have learned that when I'm not feeling well, or when my physical fitness is less than the way I want it to be, I'm motivated to change the condition. Feeling that my health is robust — that I'm well, fit, toned, strong and energetic — most definitely leads to positive feelings about myself.

Some things, like your height or bone structure, you have no control over. But you are in charge of much of your appearance: your weight, body shape and tone, complexion, hair, and general glow that comes with good health. The first key to a good physical condition is to monitor your diet and nutrition.

> "When your body is fit and healthy, you always feel good about yourself."

The Role of Diet and Nutrition

As health experts say, "We are what we eat." Good health depends on a balanced diet. A deficiency of certain vitamins, minerals, and nutrients can upset body chemistry. Any diet that emphasizes one type of food (proteins, vegetables, carbohydrates) to the exclusion of other foods may be very harmful to the body. When the body is deprived of basic nourishment, resulting in a deficiency of essential nutrients, it's more susceptible to major health breakdowns. The brain is particularly vulnerable. Recent studies indicate that excessive sugar, vitamin deficiencies, and food allergies can seriously disrupt the brain's ability to function normally and effectively.

Dietary Goals

The U.S. Senate Committee on Nutrition and Human Needs has established the following dietary goals for balanced nutrition:

- Consume only as many calories as are expended. If overweight, decrease caloric consumption and increase physical activity.
- Increase the intake of complex carbohydrates and natural sugars from about 28% to about 48% of total calories consumed.
- Reduce the intake of refined and processed sugars to account for no more than 10% of total caloric consumption.
- Reduce overall fat intake from approximately 40% to about 30% of caloric consumption.
- Reduce saturated-fat intake to account for about 10% of total caloric consumption. Balance it with polyunsaturated and monounsaturated fats, each of which should also account for about 10% of caloric consumption.
- Reduce cholesterol consumption to about 300 milligrams a day.
- Limit the intake of sodium by reducing the intake of salt to about five grams a day.

Good nutritional habits begin with your willpower to put them in place.

These goals suggest the following changes in food selection and preparation:

- Increase consumption of fruits, vegetables, and whole grains.
- Decrease consumption of refined and other processed sugars and foods high in such sugars.
- Decrease consumption of foods high in total fat, and partially replace saturated fats, whether obtained from animal or vegetable sources, with polyunsaturated fats.
- Decrease consumption of animal fat and choose lean meats, poultry, and fish.
- Substitute lowfat and nonfat milk for whole milk and lowfat dairy products for highfat dairy products.
- Decrease consumption of butterfat, eggs, and other high-cholesterol foods.
- Decrease consumption of salt and of foods with a high salt content.

Good nutritional habits begin with your willpower to put them in place. Here are some suggestions.

- **Start your day with breakfast.** If you're like most adults, you talk about the importance of having breakfast to your own children and to your students, but then maybe skip it yourself. Yet, it's so important to managing the day at hand. Just as you can't drive your car without gas, you can't have use of the brain's capabilities if it hasn't been fueled. Breakfast should consist of fruits and grains that will steadily release glucose during the day, giving fuel to the brain.

■ **Learn about nutrition.** Chances are you still think of nutrition education as the four basic food groups, information you learned when you were a child. Read the new research — thinking about nutrition has changed over the years. There are many interesting articles and books on the subject. You might want to ask your school librarian to suggest a few.

■ **Monitor your food habits.** When and why and where do you eat? Do you use food to comfort yourself? Do you eat because you are bored or depressed? Do you eat almost mindlessly, standing in front of the TV, munching away? Identify your eating habits. Keep a journal or log of all the food that you consume. Buy only those foods that are nutritious so that when you are tempted, what you eat will at least be nutritious. If you're starving first thing when you get home, you can have a healthy snack, such as fruit, before dinner.

■ **Develop a sensible diet plan.** If you decide that you need to lose weight, do it sensibly. Avoid quick fix diets; common sense is the key. Most educators pride themselves on being organized, creating and sticking to a plan — develop a formal plan for your diet. Make your meals ahead of time if possible, and have them ready for you when you come home. It lessens the temptation to reach for the potato chips.

> Write down specific, realistic goals for your fitness and wellness.

■ **Set goals for being fit and healthy.** How will you know when you've hit the target if you don't have one? A goal for fitness does not necessarily mean losing weight. It can mean learning to substitute fruit for junk food or eating one snack a day instead of three. Write down specific, realistic goals for your fitness and wellness. You might even wish to draw up a contract with yourself and enlist the help of a friend to keep you accountable.

■ **Take vitamins.** Vitamins can help improve general wellness: Vitamin B complex, magnesium, potassium, and calcium folate, for example, provide relief from fatigue and depression. A balanced diet should provide all the essential vitamins and nutrients, but taking a one-a-day vitamin tablet that contains all the essential vitamins and nutrients is also a good idea. All other doses and mega-doses of single vitamins and nutrients should be taken only on the advice of a physician.

The Role of Exercise

You are probably convinced of the advantages of exercise, and have known all along that you need to get your heart pumping a little stronger. But you may think — possibly erroneously — that you already get enough exercise just chasing around after the kids and dodging the teacher across the hall who always wants to borrow your projector. But do you?

Do you get sufficient physical activity? Many of us don't. All too often, the demands on our time and the multiplicity of our roles leave us with little time or energy for getting the proper amount of exercise required for good health. Even the amount and quality of rest needed for stamina can be shortchanged. Unfortunately, exercise seems to be the first area we ignore when our schedule becomes hectic. Yet just the opposite should be true: We should increase physical activity as a way to help dissipate stress. The benefits of exercise include:

- Increased circulation
- Assistance to the heart
- Added oxygen to the body
- Improved digestion
- Relaxed nerves, balanced emotions
- Increased resistance to disease
- Reduced fatigue
- Strengthened muscles, bones, and ligaments
- Improved figure and complexion
- Sharpened mental powers

You can take an active role in increasing your fitness through exercise.

Any one of these benefits can provide you with a good reason to exercise. Don't wait. You can take an active role in increasing your fitness through exercise. Here are some suggestions.

■ **Think fitness.** If you are fit, stay fit. If you feel that you need to work on fitness, perhaps it's time for you to get active again. Group activities are an easy way to begin. Saturdays and Sundays are a good time for outings, especially if your week is crowded and excludes opportunities for exercise. Going to the beach, camping, hiking, and bicycling can be a regular part of your time with family and friends. "Working at playing" is one way to make fitness a total part of your health routine.

■ **Challenge exercise**. Get involved in activities where you can channel the need for risk, adventure, and challenge in a productive and positive way. If you have had it with calisthenics, which do not necessarily do much for the cardiovascular system anyway, an alternative is a new fitness concept called Challenge Exercise (CE). CE adds the element of challenge to physical fitness. This challenge adds the bonus of mental well-being to the well-known euphoric experience of exercise, resulting in a degree of well-being rarely experienced after a nonchallenge exercise. It's believed that this experience, rather than the fact that exercise is good for the body, is the reason people continually return to CE sports rather than give in and let the demands of a busy schedule take priority over wellness. Examples of CE sports are swimming, skiing, surfing, horseback riding, motorcycling, bicycling, mountain and rock climbing, scuba diving, and other activities that combine a high degree of physical and mental coordination. (Non-CE sports are those such as calisthenics, jogging, or a game of golf with a motor cart.) Because of its benefits to both mind and body, CE provides an excellent means of reducing stress and of producing feelings of wellness.

■ **Team sports**. Team sports provide you with an opportunity to stay fit and have fun at the same time. Interacting with others allows you to do a lot of laughing and shouting, releasing some of your aggression and lessening stress. It would be a little odd for you to yell at the top of your lungs while jogging alone, but doing so during group activities is encouraged and is a great way to blow off steam.

You might want to encourage school-wide involvement. When I was a faculty member at Washington Irving Middle School, the entire staff would take on a particular cause together. Whether it was learning how to play badminton, or becoming a smoke-free staff, or a trim and fit staff, everyone got behind it. This involvement made activities fun and offered each participant support.

■ **Build fitness slowly and regularly**. The essential component of any effective health program is that it be aerobic in nature. Cardiovascular conditioning is dependent upon good lungs, a good heart, and physical endurance. Aerobic exercises build the body's organs wholistically, thus assisting the body in doing its work naturally.

Aerobic exercise requires you to exert a good deal of effort, but doesn't consume oxygen faster than your heart and lungs can supply it. Experts recommend three sessions of vigorous activity weekly with each session lasting from 20 to 30 minutes. These can include walking, swimming, bicycling, aerobics, jazzercise, and so on. Remember, though, to start off slowly if you're not in shape. Pick up your pace and raise your expectations as your body adjusts to your regimen.

■ **Visit your doctor.** The first step in planning your program of regular physical exercise is, of course, to see your own doctor. You should have a thorough physical examination before you embark on an exercise program of any kind. Your doctor will tell you, based upon your physical condition, just how vigorous your exercise can be.

Fitness isn't just a matter of weight control or strong muscle development. Perhaps you are trim enough, but lack tone and a sense of being healthy and vibrant. What's missing? Regular exercise. Here's where to start.

■ **Analyze and discard the excuses.** The biggest obstacle to overall fitness is the huge wall of excuses all of us must climb. These range from "There's no pool or health club in my area" to "I'm just not a jock" to (probably the most common) "I don't have the time." You don't have to go to a formal health facility to exercise; you can (for example) take a long walk — no special equipment needed. Good conditioning is more than strenuous activities; there are many exercises, such as yoga, that work on stretching rather than strength. Being fit can ward off many problems and lessen the severity of others.

■ **Develop a fun exercise program.** Exercise is most beneficial when done regularly. If you lie on the living room floor doing sit-ups and grumbling about how much you detest them, you're going to quit that exercise routine very quickly.

The essential component of any effective health program is that it be aerobic in nature.

Instead, choose one that's fun for you. It doesn't have to be something traditional like jogging; why not try ice skating (you're never too old!) or scuba diving or backpacking? Organizations like the YMCA offer short courses. Find a program that you like.

■ **Combine exercise and social time.** If you complain that you don't have enough time for exercise, why not exercise with a friend? Take a walk or ride stationary bicycles together. Apart from the motivation that having a workout partner provides, you'll be surprised at how much more time you'll be able to spend with your friends.

■ **Vary your exercises.** Athletes call this cross-training. If you swim every day, then take a hike on the weekends. If you bicycle, add roller skating or horseback riding. You'll find you are mentally refreshed by the break, and you'll be able to get a more complete fitness program if you vary the routine. Different activities use different muscles.

You'll get a more complete fitness program if you vary the routine

DISCUSSION: A Lesson Plan for Educators

1. How do you feel about your body? Are you comfortable with it, proud of it? How do your feelings about yourself physically affect you mentally and emotionally?

2. To what extent does your level of fitness serve as an example for students? If students see you looking fit and trim and talking about your racquetball game, for example, what do they learn about the value of exercise, fitness and wellness? Do students respect those educators more who take care of themselves?

3. How does low self-esteem and lack of confidence due to poor body image affect your performance as an educator? Can you trace times when you were impatient because of poor nutrition or inadequate rest? Have you ever felt your students were making fun of you because of your physique? Does your poor image of yourself cause you to shortchange your students?

Chapter 6

EMOTIONAL SECURITY:
Dealing With Fears and Insecurities

Quieting the Inner Voice of Low Self-Esteem

Emotional security is the second facet of self-esteem. Feeling emotionally secure has to do largely with understanding and dealing with our own fears and insecurities, and with feeling capable of transcending or transforming them. Educators have their share of emotional insecurities; indeed, a good number come with the territory. Many of these are interrelated and so complex that the average educator feels powerless to resolve them. The following are some of the most common fears and insecurities I have found from talking to educators around the country:

- low self-image; being "just a teacher"
- wondering whether or not one is making a positive difference in the lives of young people
- questioning skill and role competence
- failed expectations
- ego fulfillment needs that go unmet
- coping day in and day out with the low self-esteem of students
- dealing with low self-esteem fellow educators
- the uneasiness of constantly being evaluated
- the anguish that one is not doing the best for all students
- the disappointment of teaching a lesson that does not succeed
- the difficulty of covering a heavy course within the scheduled time
- the diversity of teaching methodologies and feeling that you aren't knowledgeable in using them
- the diversity of instructional materials and not having a grasp of them
- the realization of one's personal limitations in comparison with others whose outstanding abilities are so apparent
- knowing so little about the process of how children best learn
- the fear of not being able to handle the increase in teacher responsibilities and accountability
- the suspicion that students believe a teacher's impact will be minimal and inconsequential

> Emotional insecurities can be so complex that the average educator feels powerless to resolve them.

- the excessive time demands of teaching and the feeling that personal, family, recreational and social priorities are shortchanged
- the inability to participate in community affairs as much as one would like to because of increasing workload and teaching responsibilities
- changes in societal values which often make existing classroom procedures seem old-fashioned and irrelevant

Let's look a bit closer at the big issues, the turmoil they produce, and possibilities for resolution.

1. "JUST A TEACHER"

I'll never forget my first day on the job as a new teacher. My building principal, Gerald Conley, pinned a banner to the blackboard in my room that read, "Teaching is the most important profession because through the hands of teachers pass all professions." I've never forgotten that self-esteem building message. The message was more than a banner — it was the philosophy championed by all administrators in the school — it was what educators were *supposed* to take to heart, believe in, act on. Cecil Brewton and Tom Drake, the other two school administrators, spent as much time supporting teachers in embracing the right behaviors as they did students. It was one unforgettable teaching assignment. Though I became a Teacher-of-the-Year under their reign, the award belonged as much to them and my fellow colleagues as to me.

Educators *must* hold the importance of their work in the highest *esteem*.

Even though the educational profession is not regarded as highly as it once was and the public's perception of the educator has become jaded, educators *must* hold the importance of their work in the highest esteem. *Deciding that you are an educator whose charge is to shape the minds and hearts of youth, versus "just a teacher," is about upping the value of your worth in your own mind, first.*

Are You a Sissy or a Ferrari?

When the messages you send yourself are positive and esteem building, they contribute to your feelings of positive self-worth. A story of a young boy who came home crying because a classmate had called him a sissy shows how important these messages are in determining how you feel about yourself.

"Why are you crying?" his Grandma asked. "Because Paul called me a sissy! Do you think I'm a sissy, Grandma?"

"Oh no," said the grandmother. "I think you're a Ferrari."

"What?" said the boy, trying to make sense of what his grandmother had said. "Why do you think I'm a car?"

"Well, if you believe that because Paul called you a sissy, you are, you might as well believe you're a car. Why be a sissy when you can be a Ferrari!"

"Oh," exclaimed the boy gleefully, feeling quite relieved. "*I get to decide what I am!*"

This simple little story illustrates what we all need to believe: *Why be a sissy when you can be a Ferrari!*

As the grandmother knew, often the seeds of self-esteem are planted in childhood, in the formative years. A child's perception of himself is based upon what others bestow on him. A child's mind is like a recorder, storing all incoming messages. Positive or negative, these messages make up his "inner language"; they become the voice telling him what he is worth, his value. These messages (or tapes) are often played back in his adult years. Positive or negative, this inner voice is influential. Some adults respond from a wonderful and whole sense of self, while others are still responding to the negative tapes collected in their childhood when they were most receptive to someone else's perception of them.

A child's perception of himself is based upon what others bestow on him.

Just as positive statements are self-esteem building, negative statements are detrimental to self-esteem. A constant barrage of put-downs or negative self-talk takes a toll on your self-esteem.

As an educator, you constantly work to help your students see themselves as capable and confident, but what about you? What "message" do you play and how does it govern your actions? What was the basis for that inner language? When was it put in place? Asking yourself the following questions can prove to be insightful:

- Did your parents lead you to believe you were a sissy or a Ferrari?
- What did they *say* that led you to this conclusion?
- What did they *do* that led you to this conclusion?
- In your childhood, who else was instrumental in helping you shape your perception of self?
- In your early adult years, who was most instrumental in helping you shape your perception of self?
- How have you lived out these perceptions?
- Has this perception served you well? In what ways?
- What have you done in your adult years to reshape this image?
- What adult experiences have had the most positive effect on your sense of self?
- What adult experiences have had the most negative effect on your sense of self?
- If you're a sissy but you'd rather be a Ferrari, what can you do to change/transform?
- On days when you're feeling like a sissy and you'd rather be a Ferrari, what can you do to change this?

Changing or Rewriting Negative Self-Talk

Like the boy who felt bad because he had been told he was a sissy and believed it but later realized *he could decide* what he was, you can change negative self-statements into healthy ones. There's a direct connection between thoughts, feelings, and behaviors. Let's look at this in operation:

Dr. Backett approached Carol on her way to the teacher's lounge and said, "We missed you at the teacher's meeting last night, Carol. I had wanted you to talk about the new Miss School — Miss Out program. Come by my office when you get a moment, please."

Carol begins to process this message. Here are two possible scenarios of her thinking.

> **Carol's thoughts:** "Dr. Backett is upset with me. He thinks I should have been at the meeting last night. He's treating me like a child, like a student, as if I need an excused absence. This is the first meeting I've missed all year. How dare he try to make me feel guilty about it!"
>
> **Carol's feelings:** Irrational, angry, upset, defensive.
>
> **Carol's behavior:** She avoids going to Dr. Backett's office because she "wants to show him!"

Here, Carol assumes that it's Dr. Backett who made her upset and that she is justified in being defensive. She reasons that his notice of her absence is a criticism of her absence. Her thoughts affect her behavior in a negative way. A different and more positive scenario on Carol's part might be as follows.

> **Carol's thoughts:** "I am flattered that Dr. Backett wanted my input. He must value my knowledge to make a point of noticing my absence like this. It's good to be appreciated; some teachers are taken for granted."
>
> **Carol's feelings:** Rational, flattered, valued.
>
> **Carol's behavior:** She goes to Dr. Backett's office, confident about having a productive conversation with him.

Now that you're aware of how inner thoughts work for or against you, you'll want to be able to change the negative thoughts to positive ones. One way to do this is with a procedure called *thought-stopping*. What you do is visualize a stop sign whenever you start telling yourself limiting statements. This cue acts as a signal to stop thinking dysfunctional thoughts. When you catch yourself being

You can change negative self-statements into healthy ones.

negative, for example, you might literally talk to yourself, saying something like, "C'mon now, I'm not going to be down on myself. Just because this didn't work out the way I planned doesn't mean I can't generate a better alternative." The last phase of thought-stopping involves thought-substitution. Here, you would generate as many positive thoughts as possible, for example:

■ Just because Dr. Backett commented on my absence doesn't mean he is saying I was wrong for missing the meeting.

■ It shows that he notices me and my work and values what I do.

■ _____

■ _____

Rescripting Messages

Another way to turn a negative thought into a positive one is by reshaping it, by rewriting it for the desired result — for the way you wish it could be. This is often referred to as *rescripting*.

> **Example:** "I don't like my fourth period class."
>
> **Rewrite:** "I enjoy all my classes except fourth period. My fourth hour class isn't doing as well as they could be. I notice that my students seem lethargic, and I am a bit, too. I wonder if it has to do with the way the class is currently structured? I know how difficult it must be for my students to come back from lunch to a lecture type of format, especially when I have so many reluctant learners who need special assistance and who lack motivation in the first place."

Just as a student who thinks that he's not a good student will find school difficult (and this will contribute to his not liking school), your view of the situation colors it as well. When you send mostly positive messages to yourself, you bolster your self-esteem, and you start an invigorating and contagious success cycle that contributes to your performance and productivity and lends itself to an empowering presence in your relationships with students and colleagues.

Developing a positive inner language is a powerful way to enhance self-esteem.

Developing A Positive Inner Language

Developing a positive inner language is a powerful way to enhance self-esteem. Negative messages only serve to defeat you: "I can't" or "I'm just a teacher" obviously do little to promote a positive sense of self. When so many others seem to be putting down educators, the profession, and students, we needn't do it to ourselves. Here's a way to build a positive inner language.

■ **Use positive language.** Assess the kind of language *you* use. Is it positive and enabling, supportive and encouraging? What is the nature of your language to yourself, your students, and your colleagues? Do you encourage them and build their self-esteem? Do they hear that they're worthwhile and capable? Are your words and actions conveying acceptance?

■ **Label the language.** Use *terms* to depict positive esteem-building language and to differentiate it from language that undermines a positive sense of self. Call positive language "fuzzies" or "compliments," or whatever. Label inappropriate language as "zingers" or "put-downs." Identifying these polarities provides a reference point reminding you (and others) to project positive self-statements. If someone makes a put-down statement say, "That's a zinger" or "That's a put-down." When an esteem-building comment comes your way say, "That's a nice compliment!" or "Oh, that felt good! Thanks for the support!"

> When someone uses negative language excessively, gently but assertively call them on it.

■ **Insist on positive language from others.** Insist on positive language from everyone in your classroom and school environment, and yes, from fellow staff members as well. Again, the most obvious place to start is with *your* language. Don't talk negatively about yourself or others, and request the same from them. When someone uses negative language excessively, gently but assertively call them on it. For example, if a fellow educator harshly criticizes a student, say, "Some students have been dealt a bad deck of cards. I'm sure if we look we'll find this student has a lot going for him (or her). Let's just support this guy and see if we can help him build his self-esteem so he can become the good student we want him to be," or something to that effect. Look for the cup half full as opposed to half empty. High self-esteem educators appreciate your proactive approach, which involves speaking well of students as opposed to belittling them, and respect you for it.

■ **Reinforce positive statements.** Some educators (and students) have used put-down statements for so long that they have actually conditioned themselves to say the negative. If you're in the habit of using negative self-talk, catch yourself and immediately convert the negative statement to a positive one. Then, acknowledge your new behavior. You might silently say, "That's good. I'm getting to be less negative."

■ **Get in the habit of complimenting others.** Statements like, "I appreciate it when you . . .," "I feel good about myself when I . . .," "I really like it when you . . .," "Thank you . . .," "Thanks . . .," "Thanks for noticing . . .," or "When you help me I feel . . .," are common courtesy, and teach others to be complimentary in return.

2. DO I *REALLY* MAKE A DIFFERENCE?

Educators want to know that they are truly making a difference in their students' lives. Children spend a significant amount of time as well as their most formative years in the school environment. Educators are all too well aware of this and want to be a significant link in helping students develop the skills and attitudes that will lead to their being happy and capable now, and to living a functional and satisfying adult life later.

There's a difference between getting a high school diploma and a meaningful education. When educators feel young people may not be fully prepared to meet their future, they worry that they have shortchanged their students, especially in two areas:

Preparing for productive work. Perhaps today more than ever before young people face a world of increasing choices, options, and limitless possibilities. This presents them with a greater need to make appropriate choices. The more choices and decisions a person needs to make, the greater their need for high self-esteem.

Preparing for a balanced lifestyle. In addition to acquiring the skills of reading, writing, and learning, young people need valuable *self-knowledge*. Living a principle-centered existence means that students must know and value productive and meaningful work based on inner desires and talents. They must become capable of entering into mutually satisfying and loving relationships, those in which they will not be hurt emotionally or physically, nor hurt the people whom they love. They must place a high value on good health and know how to sustain wellness. They must be responsible, value happiness, care for their emotional well-being, learn to be compassionate people, be able to nurture and sustain the warmth of friendships, set and achieve *worthwhile* goals, and so much more. We want our students to be able to live a life characterized by meaning and joy. How can this be done when there appears to be few if any values that support such teachings and learnings within the regular school curriculum? Feeling that it may not be possible to arm their students with important life skills that make such a difference in the quality of their lives can cause educators to wonder if their work really makes a significant contribution to their students.

> We want our students to be able to live a life characterized by meaning and joy.

3. FAILED EXPECTATIONS

Most educators are idealists, or at least they start out that way. Newly trained educators fully believe that they are going to make a difference in the lives of young people. *To make a difference* — to do something purposeful with one's life — is a factor motivating those who train to become educators. These teacher candidates believe that all the hard work and effort will be worthwhile. Sometimes these expectations are met with success, other times they are tempered with the realization that you can't change the lives and hearts of *all* students, especially those youth who have become hard-core. The educator in an impossible assignment, and the educator who is continuously clashing head on with youth who can't be turned on or turned around, begins to wonder if she's cut out to be a teacher.

Shattered expectations make for a disheartening realization and lower self-esteem. Working with the low self-esteem student where the educator seldom sees rewards for his hard work and efforts most definitely tests his self-esteem.

Working With the Low Self-Esteem Student

Often educators will ask me *how* they can withstand working with the low self-esteem student without it taking a toll on their own self-esteem. Some educators question if building the self-esteem of a very negative child can be accomplished. Yes, it can. Working with a hard-to-like, tough-to-work-with and sometimes ungrateful student needn't always take a negative toll.

It won't be easy (you knew that!), and you can't turn a child's self-esteem around overnight. It will take a dedicated educator and a support staff nearly the entire school year to turn the poor self-image of a student into a positive one. Just as your self-esteem cannot be healthy one day and then completely diminished by the events that happen the next, neither can a poor image be turned into a positive one overnight. Though it takes time, you can change a low self-image into a positive and healthy one. Here's why.

You can't turn a child's self-esteem around overnight.

Let's say that your administrator (whose reputation as a former teacher was that of being a good educator) makes a statement implying that you aren't a very effective teacher. You know that you haven't been giving it your all. You decide to take stock. You notice that a number of students aren't doing so well — several seem to disrespect you, a few cut your class regularly, a good number of students aren't living up to their potential. There are other signs indicating things aren't going so well. The "good" teachers hang out together, and you don't seem to be accepted into that "elite" group; in fact, they seem to ignore you when you are around. Your last performance review was marginal at best. Yes, there seems to be a problem all right: You believe that you must be a terrible teacher. Then one day I stop into your classroom for a few minutes and tell you you are a brilliant teacher. Will you believe me? Probably not. My comments will be met with disbelief.

Likewise, if a child has been getting years of feedback telling him that he's a behavior problem, a worthless good-for-nothing, and it can be confirmed just by adding up the number of times he's been removed from classes, been in fights, failed courses, and so on, then his feelings of self-worth are justifiably low.

Have You Met Bill?

In looking over your new group of students you notice Bill, a student with a bad attitude, poor grades, and a real tough-looking group of friends. He's had years of practice at failing (except at being a tough guy — his friends confirm for him that he succeeds in that area). Now you come along and want to change his expectations of himself. You tell him that he "has potential" and can do good work if he'll just "apply himself." You remind him that he doesn't have to be the school bully. Naturally, your projection of his new and improved self will be met with disbelief. Not only is it unbelievable to him, but funny as well. He's serious when he calls you crazy.

You intuitively know there are tough times ahead — what do you do? It depends on your self-esteem. When confronted with a student like Bill, do you follow the actions of teacher A, C-, or F? How you respond depends on your self-esteem.

Teacher A observes Bill during the first few weeks of class, taking note of his low self-esteem as a possible cause for his uncooperative behavior and reluctance to be a good student. She sees potential in Bill and commits herself to helping him see it too. She sets out a plan of action that includes staying positive even when he is not; she "gets in his face," as students call it, setting goals and expectations for Bill, and then diligently insists that he adhere to them. His aloof and obstinate behavior does not rock her resolve to hold him accountable.

Teacher C- observes this low self-esteem student, decides she will work with him to improve his self-esteem, but when he rejects her efforts, she decides Bill isn't worth the time and attention. After all, there are so many other students, and so little time as it is.

Teacher F observes Bill and at the outset decides she will not spend her time on a student so unwilling to focus on his role as a student. She checks with the counseling office to see if she can get him referred to a special classroom or placed with another teacher "who works so well with kids like Bill." If that doesn't work, she will let him stay in class as long as he is quiet and doesn't disturb the other students, or her.

Needless to say, Bill's only chance of emerging with a positive self-esteem is with teacher A. Why? Because under her care and rigor, Bill won't get a chance to inflict his low self-esteem behaviors on himself or others for very long. She will work with him and encourage him to confront the areas that reinforce his low self-esteem, and she will help him to construct a new paradigm of himself. Rather than seeing him as a loser, and giving him yet more reinforcement as a failure, teacher A will demand that the student see himself through a different and more positive lens. She works diligently to enlist his support in putting in place a plan for doing so. Teacher A will be his lifeline to creating a new reality.

I'm not implying that Bill's low self-esteem can be transformed into a positive one with three quick strokes. It will *not* be an easy year for teacher A. In fact, it will be downright difficult for her. That's because as Bill decides to rethink his image now as one of being capable and worthy, he'll have to test the boundaries of her guidelines to see if the teacher really means it. The more dedicated she is to her cause, the more he will resist. He thinks (and his actions display it), "Surely she will give up on me like mom, dad, step-parent, friend, teacher C- and/or F did! Surely the teacher isn't serious! How could anyone believe in me — I don't!"

But one day — months later — he too will believe that he is capable and worthy. The lesson he has learned will be an unforgettable one of tenacity, courage, responsibility, respect, caring, and honor. One thing is for sure: *he will never forget this teacher.* He will esteem her and hold her in the highest of honor throughout his lifetime. He will pay tribute to her when he accepts the honors and recognitions that others bestow on him — and there will be many. Most remarkably —

Teacher A will demand that the student see himself through a different and more positive lens.

because nothing gained is lightly won — he will be forever changed. He will aspire to and achieve whatever he decides to do. He will give lectures to his children and employees based on what he learned during the trials and tribulations in which this educator worked on *rehabilitating* him. The "Bills" succeed in life.

What the Research Says About Difficult Children (This Will Make You Feel Good!)

Helping others became a major factor in turning their lives around.

In a study spanning twenty years, psychologist Emmy Werner and a team of physicians, nurses, social workers, and psychologists followed the development of nearly a thousand children, one-third of whom had experienced a difficult and turbulent childhood. Of those, one in five developed serious problems by the age of seventeen. By late adolescence, 15% had a record of serious or repeated delinquency. Most of the children in the study, however, did not get into trouble. The researchers were deeply impressed by the resiliency of the overwhelming majority of these children. Even among the high-risk children — those who had records and who showed at least four risk factors by age ten — one-fourth developed into stable, mature, and competent young adults.

How did these resilient children differ from their more troubled peers? The most striking characteristic that emerged was that they had been "underdogs" fortunate enough to have someone who cared enough to get involved. What's even more interesting is that because these children had attention paid to them even in the face of adversity, they were able to lend emotional support and help others in need — they became "care-givers." Helping others (personal responsibility) became a major factor in turning their lives around. Later, as adults, these same persons expressed a higher degree of satisfaction in helping others (social responsibility) than did those who did not have caretaking responsibilities while growing up.

Other studies confirm similar results. A long-term Harvard study, begun some forty years ago in an effort to understand juvenile delinquency, followed the lives of nearly 500 teenage children, many of whom were from impoverished or broken homes. When the subjects were compared at middle age, one fact stood out: regardless of intelligence, family income, ethnic background, or amount of education, those who had responsibilities and had been accountable for their actions enjoyed more productive lives than those who had not. They earned more money and enjoyed more job satisfaction. They had better marriages and closer relationships with their children; they had more productive and satisfying relationships with co-workers. They were healthier and lived longer. Above all, they were far happier.

4. AM I MEETING THE NEEDS OF MY STUDENTS?

A growing concern among many educators is that the classroom experience sometimes falls short in preparing students to face the demands of the outside world. Many educators fear that the range of interests and abilities in a class covers so wide a spectrum, that it's impossible to meet students' individual needs.

Furthermore, there's the question as to whether or not current evaluation methods are accurately assessing the various levels of student development, or current enough given the pace of constantly changing curricula and teaching methods. In talking with a number of education experts recently at *Fortune Magazine's* Education Summit in Washington, they concur: Our tests and measurement systems are outdated.

Apprehensions about whether or not the profession can police itself and self-correct in time to be of use to students can cause educators to question the relevancy of what they are teaching. The good teacher wonders, "Am I really effective? Am I meeting the needs of my students?"

5. AM I REALLY EFFECTIVE?

There are many ways to teach. Students learn at different rates, and in different ways. What works for one educator may not work for another. If you compare the teaching styles of each educator chosen as their state's Teacher-of-the-Year, you will find that these effective educators possess different personalities and use a variety of teaching methods and styles, but they share certain characteristics that make them effective in their roles. Among them:

■ **Effective educators don't write off any student.** Good teachers don't have one set of standards for good students and lower standards for others. They know that students learn at different rates. While some students are quicker than others, some need more help in the learning process. Good teachers are convinced that *all students can learn.* These educators believe that it's their job to see that all students reach not only the course proficiency requirements, but fulfill their potentials. They set high expectations for their students, knowing that students who are expected to do well in school usually succeed.

Good teachers are convinced that all *students* can learn.

■ **Effective educators know the importance of praise as a motivator.** Effective educators don't take for granted good behavior or success, nor do they comment only on misbehavior or failure. Successful teachers continually encourage their students and provide experiences where each student can enjoy a measure of success.

■ **Effective educators create an atmosphere conducive to learning.** Warmth for their students and enthusiasm for the subjects taught often go together. Good educators make subjects come alive and, simultaneously, make all students feel appreciated and cared about.

■ **Effective educators use class time well.** Good teachers develop creative and stimulating lesson plans, and *through a series of teaching methodologies*, test for teaching and learning outcomes. They know that if a student isn't learning, they need to find alternative ways in which the student *does* succeed at learning.

■ **Effective educators establish clear boundaries for student behavior.** Good teachers make only those rules that are necessary, and are consistent and fair when reinforcing them.

■ **Effective educators seize learning opportunities.** Good teachers encourage all students to contribute in class and create a cooperative learning environment. They are flexible and willing to move the class in a new direction if it seems to be more understandable and interesting to the students. They stay open to new ideas and learn from their students.

■ **Effective educators have a clearly defined philosophy.** Good teachers know that in order to focus on those things that are of most value, they need to have clarified a philosophy that serves to guide their actions.

We need to feel our efforts are appreciated and valued.

6. I WANT MORE RESPECT AND ADMIRATION

Teaching is serving others. In teaching others, we give of ourselves — we express our interest and caring for our students. We need to feel our efforts are appreciated and valued. Do you feel:

- ■ respected and admired by your students?
- ■ respected and admired by your colleagues?
- ■ respected and admired by your administrators?
- ■ respected and admired by the parents of your students?
- ■ respected and admired by the support staff?
- ■ respected and admired in your role as an educator by your family members?

Unfortunately, being an educator no longer commands the respect and admiration it once did. Once upon a time educators were revered as the smartest people in town, the fountainhead of knowledge! Not only has the information explosion rendered that position impossible, but the *rate* of change has too.

Educators seem to be getting less and less respect from a number of factions — parents, administrators, students, the media, and peers. If a good number of educators don't feel esteemed in their schoolplace, still others suffer from the feeling that they are not especially esteemed as community leaders either. Nor do educators get sufficient appreciation from students or their colleagues. Added to this is the severe shortage of stroking from those in positions of authority — causing educators to wonder if they are effective and valued, or if they have chosen their careers wisely. Then there's the shortage of money and the effects of accelerating inflation which make salary increases inadequate. The statements, "I'm *just* a teacher" and "I feel like I'm just babysitting," are echoed by more and more educators.

No one big movement is going to come along to improve the image of the profession. What can *you* do to garner more status and respect? Here are a few suggestions. Discuss these as a faculty, and add your own ideas.

■ **Conduct yourself like a professional.** Your conduct is central to being perceived as a professional. Do you want to be treated as a professional? Be one. Be good at your work. Read the journals of your trade. Either subscribe to one or two such journals, or check them out from your school's teacher resource center or from the local public library. If your school doesn't get these professional magazines for the staff, suggest they do.

Stay current in your field. Know your curriculum content, network with others in your core area, exchange ideas on how to teach your subject matter in a way that piques the curiosity of your students. There is no substitute for a competent, exciting, and challenging teacher. It's your profession; it's your job. Do it well.

If you have major concerns about the way things are being done at your school, don't merely complain and give excuses. Be proactive. Be an advocate for changing what needs reform. Enlist the support of others. Then get involved to bring your ideas to fruition. This includes speaking positively about your students and colleagues and school, and presenting yourself with pride when representing your school in any endeavor, whether at a PTA meeting or out of town on a conference. It also extends to the seemingly smaller things, such as asking that students address you by your last name, *not* by your first name. Children are young people in need of models.

Be an advocate for changing what needs reform.

■ **Think of yourself as a professional.** Getting status and respect is dependent upon your commanding it. If you think of yourself as "just a teacher," chances are, you'll be accorded that way. Project what you want to come back to you in the way of respect. Think of yourself as a professional. Educators are leaders. They are also specialists in child development, in teaching and learning outcomes, in counseling children, in working with parents and psychologists.

■ **Have a "business card" made up.** More and more educators now carry a business card. It's a great idea. You can get several hundred business cards printed up for as little as $25. Your business card should carry the name of your school district, your school's name and address, your name, and other pertinent information, such as the grade and subject you teach. Use them with parents. What parent doesn't need to have the phone number of his child's school, to remember the educator's name, and to feel that you (their child's teacher) are a professional doing a job? Use your card to exchange and network with other educators; use it as a public relations tool in your normal dealings outside of the schoolplace. Use it to remind yourself of your status as an educator. Respect yourself, and act accordingly.

■ **Dress like a pro.** Dress the part. It's hard to think of someone doing a serious job in an important career when you look like you should be out in your garden! Only you know what "professional look" is right for your school and city. The point is, look like you consider you and your position important when you get dressed for work each day.

7. I DEAL WITH CONFLICTING EDUCATIONAL PHILOSOPHIES, PRACTICES, AND VALUES

The flux and flow of conflicting educational philosophies and practices within members of the same faculty, and of trying to cope with the plurality of values and attitudes can be troubling and trying. It's not just the practices and values of the staff:

Many educators feel that students are not receptive towards basic values.

Many educators feel that their students are not receptive toward those values the educator considers basic to personal growth and social responsibility. More and more educators perceive that young people today all too often disparage tradition, knowledge, achievement, standards of excellence, and hard work, and they fear that students will graduate with a value system inadequate to cope responsibly with the moral issues of life.

Educators may also experience the inner conflict of trying to balance their personal beliefs with the socially accepted norms parents expect teachers to epitomize, coupled with the fear of teaching either too quixotic or too pragmatic guidelines (for example, teaching "up" to inner city children who may become discouraged rather than encouraged by extremely high standards, or teaching "down" to those same children because of the erroneous belief that they cannot come up to higher standards). Another growing concern among educators is that their own ethnic background is so different from their students' as to make a common frame of reference difficult.

DISCUSSION: A Lesson Plan for Educators

1. How can educators identify their own emotional insecurities and fears? How can we determine whether these fears are rational and have a logical basis, or are illogical? Are fears ever appropriate? How can we use these fears to challenge ourselves to become better educators?

2. Have we been lulled into thinking that teaching is a second-rate career? What are examples of ways in which we put our career down without realizing we are doing so, or let others put us down for being educators?

3. How can we identify our own deeply held beliefs and values? Do these values change over time, or are they so ingrained that they are constant? How can we identify our students' values? Is part of our job to instill our values in our students? Is it reasonable to expect that of us? What do we do when our values and culture clash with those of our students?

4. How can educators rewrite negative self-talk? What should they "say"?

Chapter 7

EMOTIONAL SECURITY:
Dealing With the Stress and Strain of the Profession

Stress — An Occupational Hazard

Virtually no one feels free of stress these days, certainly not classroom educators with too much to do and too little time to do it. Because they are working with too many students, many with special learning needs — be it gifted or limited — some of whom have very complex emotional needs, hardly a day goes by when educators are not stretched to capacity. In today's educational arena, stress seems to be an accepted part of the professional's life, an "occupational hazard." That does not mean, however, that you must accept and suffer the resulting mental anguish and physical consequences produced by stress.

Stress! Everyone experiences stress, but what *is* it? How does it affect you and those around you? What *causes* it? What can be done to manage stress, to moderate its negative effects? Can stress be used to your *advantage*? Given the nature of your work, how can you continue to be effective day after day, year after year, remaining at peak performance — without burning out? How does stress affect your productivity?

How violently or calmly we respond to stress itself is under *our* control.

Understanding Stress

The concept of stress means something different to each of us. The business person may think of it as frustration or emotional tension, the air-traffic controller as a problem in concentration, the biochemist as a purely chemical event, the athlete as muscular tension, the parent as an overwhelming and demanding schedule, the small child as a stomachache. You, the classroom educator, may think of it as a discipline problem with a fractious student or a demanding or irate parent, the frustration of having too much paperwork take away from your actual teaching time, or something else entirely. While stress is no more than anxiety or physical nervousness to some individuals, in others it can lead to emotional despair. What is stressful for someone else may not be to you.

Each of us responds in different ways to stress-producing factors. How violently or calmly we respond to stress itself is under *our* control. Many professionally effective and personally powerful people recognize that the power to manage stress competently lies within themselves, thus they turn it to their advantage.

The question, then, is not whether to eliminate stress altogether (a difficult, if not impossible goal), but how to manage it — or rather, manage our *response* to it. Once you know what causes you stress and how you respond to it, you'll be better able to develop skills and strategies for minimizing and managing it.

Since you can't avoid all stress, the goal becomes to disarm its negative effects and minimize the toll it exacts from you. The bottom line is that you *must* manage it so as not to endanger the health and productivity of yourself — as well as your students and fellow colleagues. Your overall goal is to use stress constructively to lessen the toll it extracts from your health, and to promote a sense that you have control over yourself and those reactions that have the potential to be debilitating.

Stress Is a Cue to Cope, to Adapt, to Make a Change

You must manage stress so as not to endanger your health and productivity.

Very simply, stress is the name given to the reaction of the body mobilizing its defenses against any incoming perceived threat. Stress is the body's physical, mental, and chemical reaction to circumstances that cause confusion, irritation, or excitement. It results not so much from the stress-producing event itself, but rather, from the way you perceive that event and handle (process) it — therefore, stress can have either a positive or negative charge. In other words, how you perceive stress is under *your* control.

How you manage it matters. Handled poorly, stress becomes an enemy which debilitates you; at its extreme, it contributes to weakening the body and rendering it less able to ward off diseases. Handled well, it can signal the brain to release more fuel needed to provide extra strength to meet an immediate circumstance, and it can strengthen you for the next encounter. Some stress reactions are so subdued that you're not even aware of them. Others show themselves clearly in tension, heart palpitations, inability to concentrate, insomnia, headaches, muscle tension, even ulcers. Short-term stress can cause symptoms like severe headaches and stomachaches. Excessive stress on a long-term basis can cause ulcers and trigger diseases such as high blood pressure and arthritis. Unbridled stress can contribute to heart disease and the weakening of body organs.

In a very real sense, the stress response is a cue to cope — to adapt, to make a change, to prepare for action. In stressful situations, messages from the brain, acting through the hypothalamus, stimulate the sympathetic nerves and the pituitary, thus triggering an outpouring of adrenaline from the adrenal glands. Circulation speeds up, more energy-rich sugar appears in the blood, muscles tense, saliva decreases, eyes dilate, senses become more acute, the thyroid is activated, and the body's muscle function is strengthened. At the same time, blood cells are released from storage depots into the circulation, and the digestive system goes into temporary inaction. All of these reactions are designed to help the body gear up for action. When the stress situation eases, this reaction shuts down, though in periods of prolonged stress this automatic mechanism can become exhausted and a person may become more susceptible to illness.

Prolonged Stress = Burnout = Dropout

Given the nature and intensity of teaching, many educators fear that they have "burned out." Burnout is a feeling of total exhaustion. There may be a noticeable loss of the interest, thoroughness, and vitality you once brought to your work. You may care less about what others think of you or how they perceive your effectiveness; you may lose interest in your appearance; you may tolerate your sagging self-esteem without actively seeking ways to refuel it, thereby starting a downward spiral of dysfunctional or even destructive behaviors; you may stop caring about and helping your colleagues; you may lose interest in those things you once greatly enjoyed — hobbies, pastime activities, sports, reading, and so on. There may be a feeling of apathy or a general level of lingering frustration.

If you continue to experience debilitating feelings (frustration, anger, sadness, hopelessness), you may become less interested in remaining vital. Feeling overwhelmed and unable to cope can cause you to *drop out*. The dropping out may be physical in that you are frequently absent or you actually quit your job. Or it may be psychological in the sense that you start a cycle of "get-by" performances in your teaching, assign more busy work to keep the students quiet, let your aide take over more and more, or (a favorite last resort!) show more films — basically abandoning the function of interacting in the teaching/learning experience.

The toll your stress takes affects not only yourself but often contributes to the stress levels of those around you. Studies on the effects stress has on the behaviors of teachers, for example, show that educators who are under stress (real or perceived) create great amounts of stress for their students. Not only do these educators give out fewer positive reinforcements (the most effective way to change human behavior) but, in fact, give out more negative reinforcements. Stressful educators also resort to negative ways of controlling and managing student behavior.

Educators who are under stress create great amounts of stress for their students.

If you're not adept at dealing with stress effectively, and most especially if you avoid confronting it, you may stockpile the stress, letting its effects build up to intolerable levels. Eventually, you lose your idealism, the drive and motivation that led to your being entrusted with a position as an educator; you are no longer passionate about your work and your calling to teach. You in effect betray those who believe in you, those who felt you capable of helping others.

Why Is Being an Educator So Stressful?

Did you know that next to air-traffic controllers, teaching is rated as the next most stressful occupation? You probably did! There are a multitude of reasons why educators are experiencing stress and anxiety in alarming proportions. Educators often say they feel isolated and have little opportunity to interact with their colleagues. They sometimes feel physically cut off from other adults in a room filled only with students, and they long for the emotional support of others who have faced similar situations. Other reasons have to do with student apathy, inadequate preparation time, and not enough support from superiors. Some educators say that parents are less interested in their children's school and education than they used to be, that they sometimes feel alone in their concerns to assist students in learning. The reasons are numerous and differ from school to school, from educator to educator, from situation to situation, and even from day to day. Educators most frequently identify their sources of stress as:

What creates stress for you?

- ■ I have too much to do and too little time to do it.

- ■ I have too much responsibility.

- ■ I get feedback only when my performance is unsatisfactory.

- ■ I am surrounded by stress carriers: individuals who are demanding, highly anxious, indecisive, chronically critical, and depressive.

- ■ There is ambiguity or rigidity in my work.

- ■ Others I work with seem unclear about what my role is.

- ■ I frequently have to interrupt my teaching to deal with student behavior problems.

- ■ I either have constant change and daily variability or deadening stability.

- ■ Decisions or changes that affect me are made "above" me. I'm expected to carry these out even though I might not believe in them, fail to see how they relate to my school or duties, or feel unsure how to carry them out.

- ■ I must attend numerous meetings; many of them seem pointless.

- ■ I feel overqualified for the work I actually do.

- ■ I feel underqualified for the work I actually do.

- ■ I get no personal support from the people with whom I work.

- ■ I don't get enough interaction with adults.

How about you? What creates stress for you? The following inventory can help you get a better idea of what creates stress for *you*, and how you cope with it.

WHAT CREATES STRESS FOR YOU?
AN INVENTORY FOR EDUCATORS

© 1991 Bettie B. Youngs, Ph.D.

DIRECTIONS: Place a check next to those items on the inventory that are stress producing for you personally. Don't passively check something that you know your colleagues find upsetting but you individually do not. For example, some educators react very negatively to noise around them while they are working, while others associate it with student productivity, and still others manage to tune it out. Don't be lulled into thinking that some things "should" cause stress; the goal of this inventory is to help you note exactly what does, in fact, cause *you* stress.

I. DEALING/COPING WITH CHANGE

Yes   No

___ ___   1. There are always new rules, regulations and policies that require constant change and adaptation on *my* part.

___ ___   2. I must acquire new teaching skills and learn new behavior management skills to keep pace with the needs of students.

___ ___   3. After-school activities (monitoring dances, sporting events, going to PTA meetings) disrupt my daily routine and family life.

___ ___   4. I must constantly keep up with new and innovative instructional materials and curriculum to keep pace with the profession.

___ ___   5. It's difficult to keep abreast of the research in my area of expertise.

II. INTERPERSONAL BEHAVIOR

___ ___   6. I do not interact well with my colleagues.

___ ___   7. My colleagues rarely get together on a social basis.

___ ___   8. My peers and I seldom talk about areas outside of teaching, such as home and family life and outside interests and activities.

___ ___   9. There is a feeling of competition rather than cooperation among my peers.

___ ___   10. I have to confront students on a daily basis.

___ ___   11. I worry that I am not the kind of teacher my school wants and expects.

___ ___   12. My teaching style does not mesh well with the needs and expectations of my administrators (or my students).

There is a feeling of competition rather than cooperation among my peers.

III. ROLE CLARITY

Yes No

___ ___ 13. I don't know whether my primary role is as disciplinarian or teacher.

___ ___ 14. I feel pressure between spending time at work and with my family.

___ ___ 15. I feel conflict between what I must do and what my values would have me do.

___ ___ 16. The demands from students, fellow teachers, and administrators pull me in different directions.

___ ___ 17. I feel conflict between spending time dealing with student behavior versus time spent on instructional activities.

___ ___ 18. I feel overtrained; my work is not sufficiently challenging.

___ ___ 19. I do not receive clear feedback on my performance.

___ ___ 20. I don't know whether my focus should be "curriculum centered," or "child centered."

IV. COPING WITH JOB DEMANDS

___ ___ 21. I have too many areas of responsibility.

___ ___ 22. Class schedules are not realistic for what I need to accomplish.

___ ___ 23. I lack clear-cut authority to accomplish responsibilities.

___ ___ 24. I often spend nights and vacation time finishing my work.

___ ___ 25. Crisis and urgency are the norm where I work.

___ ___ 26. I feel guilty for relaxing during the school day.

I have little say in policymaking, even though I must implement it.

V. ORGANIZATIONAL CONSTRAINTS

___ ___ 27. I am restricted in my use of my own ideas and creativity in improving the educational environment.

___ ___ 28. I have little say in policymaking, even though I must implement it.

___ ___ 29. I have little, if any, say in the district's goals, and the school's plan for implementing them.

___ ___ 30. The structure of the school day is very restricting.

___ ___ 31. There are few avenues (and incentives) for promotion.

VI. THE WORKPLACE

Yes   No

___ ___ 32. My classroom is too crowded.

___ ___ 33. I have little control over the temperature in the classroom.

___ ___ 34. The classroom is noisy and disorderly.

___ ___ 35. The classroom is embarrassing (furniture, drapery/blinds are tattered and soiled).

___ ___ 36. The classroom is set up in a way that makes class discussion difficult.

___ ___ 37. Notes or pagings from the office are frequent.

___ ___ 38. The lighting is not adequate for the kind of paperwork I do.

___ ___ 39. The classroom is situated along a busy hallway, making me self-conscious because everyone who walks by peers in; I am afraid to relax and feel I always have to look busy.

___ ___ 40. I have no privacy.

Interpreting Your Results

There is no "score" on this test, no passing or failing magic number.   However, if you have a great many check marks and nodded your head vehemently throughout the test, you know that you need to take action. As you recall, the purpose of the inventory was to get you thinking about your own *personal* situation, about what causes *you* stress. This assessment is a pointer, a tool to tell you where to begin to eliminate or modify the sources of stress. The knowledge of what is causing your anxiety can help you reduce it by giving "felt" stress a definition. Rather than simply saying, "Boy, am I stressed!" you can say, "I am very stressed lately; I think it has a great deal to do with the noise level in the hall."

Once you know more precisely what is causing your stress, you can work to eliminate it. For example, the simple act of closing the door to your classroom so that you can have a quiet corner might lower your stress level significantly.

The key to managing stress is awareness and self-understanding.

The key to managing stress is awareness and self-understanding. The more you can learn about yourself, and what stressors are operating, the better chance you have to learn and grow and change in order to be effective in your role. The following stress profile for teachers is designed to help you more clearly define, on a self-scoring basis, the areas and frequency of your stress. As you read each item, evaluate the statement in terms of a period of time rather than a specific day you remember. Indicate how often the source of stress occurs by circling the number that corresponds to the frequency of occurrence. Do not read the stress profile scoring sheet until after you have completed all items.

STRESS PROFILE FOR EDUCATORS

© 1991 Bettie B. Youngs, Ph.D.

PART I
Resistance to Stress

DIRECTIONS: Respond to each of the following with a scoring range of 1 to 5, with a 1 meaning Very Often and a 5 meaning Very Rarely. Remember, answer as honestly as possible according to your own situation. Don't answer based on what you think you *should* be doing, but on what you are actually like now.

___ 1. I'm less than 10 pounds overweight or underweight.

___ 2. I eat at least one sit-down, relaxed meal a day and have a well-balanced diet.

___ 3. I exercise at least 20 minutes a day, three days a week, doing an aerobic exercise that increases my heartbeat.

___ 4. I get about eight hours sleep a night most nights.

___ 5. I drink fewer than three cups of caffeinated drinks (coffee, tea, soft drinks) a day.

___ 6. I drink no more than two or three alcoholic drinks a week.

___ 7. I smoke very little, usually fewer than five cigarettes a day.

___ 8. I consider myself in general good health and have no specific health worries.

___ 9. I make a point of taking a few minutes a day for "downtime," time to relax and unwind.

___ 10. I make a point of doing at least one activity a day just for me, something I enjoy.

___ 11. I make enough money to cover my living expenses and have no serious financial worries.

___ 12. I have a close or best friend with whom I can discuss my day on a regular basis.

___ 13. I have a wide variety of interesting friends and acquaintances with whom I do fun activities.

___ 14. I belong to a club or social organization that makes me feel accepted and wanted.

___ 15. I have good communication with my family or with the people in my household; we can talk out little annoyances before they become serious problems.

___ 16. I have a supportive family and know I can count on my relatives to help if I were ever in serious trouble.

> I make a point of taking a few minutes a day to relax and unwind.

___ 17. I am able to "blow up" and get matters off my chest, but then forget the matter and go on relatively easily.

___ 18. I am able to give and take love and affection.

___ 19. I have at least one person in my life who tells me regularly that he or she loves me.

___ 20. I am comforted by my spiritual beliefs/faith.

SCORING: Add up the numbers you assigned to each statement. Subtract 20. If your total is under 30, congratulations! You have a strong resistance to stress and are probably handling the events in your life well. If your total is between 31 and 50, you are vulnerable to stress, and should be more aware of what stressors are in your life and how well or poorly you handle them. If your score is over 51, you are extremely vulnerable to stress and need to reevaluate your life-style, or possibly talk with someone such as a counselor to help you get better balance in your life.

PART II
Negative Stressors for Teachers

DIRECTIONS: In the left-hand column, list five things about your job that you do not like, things that cause you stress. At first, list them as they come to you. Then go back and assign priorities to each item: which causes you the most stress, which causes you the least. List them in order of the most stressful to the least stressful in the second column.

_____	# 1	_____
_____	# 2	_____
_____	# 3	_____
_____	# 4	_____
_____	# 5	_____

ANALYSIS: Did you have trouble thinking of five, or could you have gone on and on? You may find it interesting to note what educators list as their Top Ten:

1. Paperwork
2. Administration
3. Nonteaching duties
4. Low pay
5. Dealing with parents/community
6. Student apathy
7. Discipline
8. Other teachers
9. No time to accomplish tasks
10. Work load

What is upsetting for one individual may not be for another.

Chances are, you had some of these on your own list. However, you may not have listed others, not considering them stressful. Keep in mind that what is upsetting for one individual may not be for another. In fact, one teacher's stressor is another teacher's fun . . . as indicated by the next part of the profile.

PART III
Positive Stressors for Teachers

When the word "stress" is mentioned, most people immediately think of its negative aspects. But some stress can be positive. For example, juggling a career, family, social life, and self, or getting married, are certainly stressful, as are getting a promotion, losing weight, and seeing your child give her first piano recital. Yet depending on how you look at them, all of these can be desirable experiences. Some stressors can be advantageous and just plain fun. Try the following exercise:

Some stressors can be advantageous and just plain fun.

DIRECTIONS: Following along the lines of the previous exercise, list those five things about your job that you do like and find satisfying and/or exciting. At first, just jot the items down in no particular order. Do this in the first column. Then go back and assign priorities.

	# 1	
	# 2	
	# 3	
	# 4	
	# 5	

ANALYSIS: Perhaps the only thing more subjective than dislikes is likes. Below are what educators list as their Top Ten. How many of these did you list?

1. Working with students
2. Colleagues
3. Summer vacations
4. Student progress
5. Working hours

6. Subject matter
7. Freedom to implement
8. Varied workday
9. Helping others
10. Challenge

PART IV
Managing Stress

So far, you have diagnosed how vulnerable you are to stress, and thought about both negative and positive stressors that you encounter in teaching. The last part of this stress profile deals with how well you handle those stresses.

DIRECTIONS: The following statements list common stress-coping techniques, both positive and negative. Put a **YES** or **NO** by each statement as it applies to you.

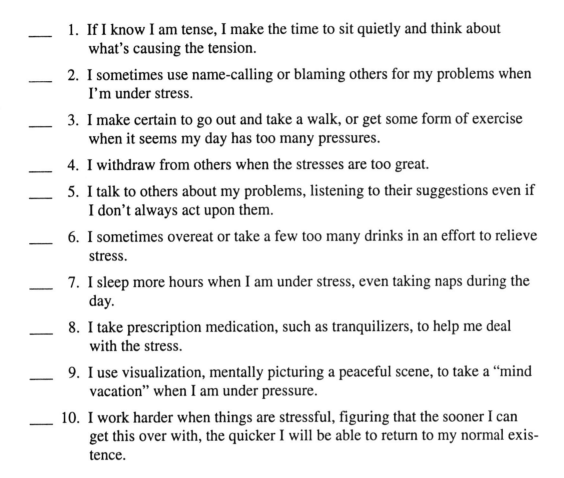

___ 1. If I know I am tense, I make the time to sit quietly and think about what's causing the tension.

___ 2. I sometimes use name-calling or blaming others for my problems when I'm under stress.

___ 3. I make certain to go out and take a walk, or get some form of exercise when it seems my day has too many pressures.

___ 4. I withdraw from others when the stresses are too great.

___ 5. I talk to others about my problems, listening to their suggestions even if I don't always act upon them.

___ 6. I sometimes overeat or take a few too many drinks in an effort to relieve stress.

___ 7. I sleep more hours when I am under stress, even taking naps during the day.

___ 8. I take prescription medication, such as tranquilizers, to help me deal with the stress.

___ 9. I use visualization, mentally picturing a peaceful scene, to take a "mind vacation" when I am under pressure.

___ 10. I work harder when things are stressful, figuring that the sooner I can get this over with, the quicker I will be able to return to my normal existence.

SCORING: For each odd-numbered question, give yourself +1 point for each **YES** and –1 point for each **NO**. For even-numbered questions, give yourself –1 point for each **YES** and +1 point for each **NO**. You might have a 0 score, with the good and bad coping strategies cancelling each other out. Any positive score is good (the higher the positive, the better). A negative score indicates a problem area.

This stress profile took you through three steps. First, you diagnosed your own level of vulnerability to see how susceptible you are to stress. Then you diagnosed your own stressors, positive and negative. Finally, you evaluated how well or poorly you are currently coping with stress. The goal of this profile is to make you aware of how you are doing now in order to help you prepare to deal better with stress in the future. Knowing what causes stress for you can help you develop skills and select strategies for decreasing stress in your life.

Coping With Stress

Being stress-free does not mean living a life absent of conflict, but rather, that you possess the ability to cope — you have mastery over stressful situations. Those individuals who are flexible enough to adapt to the stressors around them

Being stress-free does not mean living a life absent of conflict.

seem to fare better, take themselves less seriously, and lead a more balanced life. There are a number of ways to alleviate stress.

- Start your day by taking 15 minutes of quiet time to get organized, then prioritize the things you must get done that day.

- Schedule "off limits" time when you need it.

- Eat breakfast each day.

- Express your feelings clearly and in a straightforward way.

- Plan downtime or idletime every day.

- Concentrate on one task at a time so you can enjoy your accomplishments.

Interact at least once a day with someone in your school who makes you laugh.

- At least three days a week, make a pact with your fellow teachers at the lunch table that you won't "talk shop." Steer the discussion into personal matters or solve the problems of the world (world hunger, pollution, corruption); stay clear of your more immediate problems (class size, budget cutbacks).

- Avoid sitting with negative teachers — those who create stress.

- Spend time thinking (or talking) about what you like about your job.

- Practice mini-mind vacations where you visualize a scene that is especially comforting to you for five minutes each day.

- Interact at least once each day with someone in your school who makes you laugh.

- Think about involvement in outside activities that provide personal satisfaction.

- Plan a free weekend every other weekend.

- Avoid situations where you have prolonged waits. For example, if going out to dinner, go before or after the usual dinner crowd.

- Develop a vacation attitude after work (treat your home as your vacation home).

- Live by the calendar, not the stop watch.

- Plan easy-going, non-structured vacations, three to four days in duration.

- Get involved with a friend, your spouse, or a child in an activity that will teach you new concepts, new skills, or new processes.

- Devise a three-times-per-week, 20-minute physical activities schedule — like jumping rope or riding a stationary bike.

One concept central to managing stress is to recognize the role expectations play in giving a person either a feeling of gratification or frustration. Whether you call your work exhausting or exciting depends largely upon your own attitude. You need to be on friendly terms with your work and your life.

You can also dissipate stress by an act of will, by placing yourself mentally at a distance and looking at the stressful situation dispassionately, then deliberately see the humorous side and laugh. It's one of the greatest secrets: to take yourself and your importance in the total scheme of things less seriously than a person ordinarily does. Yet an important judgment enters in: The need to recognize that sometimes a single individual makes the critical difference in the outcome of an event. Intuition tells you when to take yourself seriously, and when not to.

Other possibilities that can reduce the amount of stress educators experience in the profession include the following:

- Improve in-service workshops and teacher preparation education.

- Form cadres of teacher researchers who are assigned to work on problems related to the profession.

- Revitalize your career periodically — to change those activities you dislike and improve those activities you enjoy.

- Consider a sabbatical — write to curriculum groups, to exchange programs, to the state department of education, to federal grant-giving agencies or other organizations to determine your options.

- Visit other schools and classrooms during the school year.

- Teach at a university in a summer program.

- Hire older students to do routine clerical work.

- Elect a preretirement plan.

- Make your classroom attractive. Try growing something green (not mold!). Put an area rug on the floor. Hang some of your favorite pictures. Get a bookcase that doesn't look like it was issued by the army. Bring in some sound (other than the students), get a radio or stereo. You spend a great deal of time in your classroom, so make it pleasant.

- Avoid mean and stupid people. I know I'm not supposed to say that, but you must admit there are always a couple of staff members you just can't please and who just won't participate. After you've tried to bolster their self-esteem and you find they won't return the gesture, stay clear of them. They'll dislike you no more or less. In fact, they may have something real to deal with.

On a final note, don't be hesitant to seek professional assistance if necessary. Although many stress-related symptoms clear up when the stressor is removed or the emotional difficulty subsides, chronic problems may require the attention of a specialist. Severe depression or overwhelming work, family or emotional problems, drug or alcohol abuse are examples of problems that should be dealt with

Whether you call your work exhausting or exciting depends largely upon your own attitude.

under the guidance of a professional. A counselor will not tell you how to live your life, but he or she can provide guidelines to follow in evaluating your situation. Through tests and questionnaires administered by a skilled professional in the area of stress, you can learn what health concerns loom; through counseling, you can learn how best to reduce those hazards.

Strategies for managing stress can be learned.

You needn't always succumb to stress; you needn't always let it debilitate you. Strategies for managing stress can be learned. By developing skills and selecting strategies for decreasing stress, you increase your psychological heartiness and increase your resilience. If managing stress is an area of concern for you, you may want to attend a stress management workshop to learn effective coping strategies. You can also begin to read up on the subject. Books like *A Stress-Management Guide for Educators* can be very helpful in learning to identify the source of your stress and in finding ways to successfully manage it. The suggested reading section at the end of this book lists this and other helpful resources. You may wish to ask the school librarian for additional information.

DISCUSSION: A Lesson Plan for Educators

1. What is stress? Can it be eliminated entirely? Is it mostly in the mind, psychosomatic? What are the symptoms of stress? How do you know when you are under stress?

2. What is an acceptable level of stress? Can stress ever be good, in other words, used as a challenge? How do various events lead to different levels of stress for different people? What causes stress, and can those causes be lessened or eliminated entirely?

3. What coping mechanisms are available for dealing with stress? Is it the role of the school to have some of these coping mechanisms available to teachers (such as support groups or professional help)? Should educators be able to recognize when their colleagues are overwhelmed with stress; is it our job to help them deal with it? What can be done on a daily basis to help lessen the effects of stress?

Chapter 8

IDENTITY:
WHO ARE *YOU?*

Getting in Touch With Yourself

Self-image is the third facet of self-esteem. When physical safety and emotional security needs are met, the WHO AM I? question (identity) — evaluating personal essence — emerges and becomes important to us.

Constructing a *realistic* self-image contributes to a *healthy* self-esteem. Sometimes we get so busy dealing with the day-to-day activities of making a living — the *having and getting* functions — especially if we have taken on a great number of roles and responsibilities, that we can neglect the *being and becoming* side of our development. The problem is that in the absence of a consciousness that honors and protects our *wholeness* we can squander our health, talents, maybe even our life. And of course, there's always the possibility of giving up our own identity, trading it in for becoming who someone else wants us to be, which in turn causes us to feel suspended from ourselves, or of living a life of quiet desperation. It's all too easy to get out of touch with *who* we are.

Looking into our own lives — gaining self-knowledge — is not being just *self-involved;* it's important that we do this. Maybe you've heard comments like, "I just need to get back in touch with my needs" or "I need some time for *me.*" "Know thyself" is good advice. When a person is out of touch with himself and his needs, he is likely to be out of touch with the needs of others. Unfortunately, all too often when someone signs out of the "rat race" to spend time with himself, we unkindly say he is having "an identity crisis."

An identity crisis can be avoided — if you put a premium on living your life in the present. *Living consciously* is a willingness to think about the choices you make, the actions you take, a willingness to examine your needs, feelings, and aspirations — so that you're not a stranger to yourself. It's a willingness to *take responsibility* for your life and well-being, for your choices and actions. It means you think about the quality of consciousness you bring to your work and relationships. It's also the willingness to treat yourself with respect, to stand up for your values and beliefs, and to lead a life whereby your behaviors are congruent with your values.

Examine your needs, feelings, and aspirations — so that you're not a stranger to yourself.

It's easy to get derailed — when the identity is weak, fragile, incomplete — the person appears a stranger to himself, the "You're okay, I'm not" syndrome. He might even undermine his own talents, diminish the fruits of his labor, feel unworthy of deserved praise, or shield himself by putting up a protective mask, as illustrated in Lee Ezell's poem, "The Paint Brush."

The Paint Brush

I keep my paint brush with me
Wherever I may go,
In case I need to cover up
So the real me doesn't show.
I'm so afraid to show you me,
Afraid of what you'll do
You might laugh or say mean things
I'm afraid I might lose you.
I'd like to remove all of my paint coats
To show you the real, true me,
But I want you to try and understand
I need you to like what you see.
So if you'll be patient and close your eyes
I'll strip off all my coats real slow,
Please understand how much it hurts
To let the real me show.
Now my coats are all stripped off
I feel naked, bare and cold,
If you still love me with all that you see
You are my friend pure as gold.
I need to save my paint brush though
And hold it in my hand,
I want to keep it handy
In case somebody doesn't understand.
So please protect me, my dear friend,
And thanks for loving me true,
But please let me keep my paint brush with me
Until I love me, too.

When you compromise your identity, your self-esteem pays the toll.

When you compromise your identity, your self-esteem pays the toll. It's not a question of "getting an identity." Everyone has an identity. The question is, what do you see, and is this image a healthy, positive one? Sometimes it is, and sometimes it isn't. Unfortunately, and all too often, a person may come to believe that his personal price tag reads "just a teacher" instead of "I'm a professional educator; I prepare children for their futures."

Sometimes your inner picture needs only minor repair; at times it needs to be fine-tuned or refocused; sometimes it needs to be replaced by an entirely new picture because it is damaged and creating problems in your life. Accurate or inaccurate, healthy or dysfunctional, your identity contributes to your inner picture of self-worth which in turn influences your actions. A teacher who sees herself in a positive light acts positively, while someone who sees herself as "just a teacher," walks, talks, and acts the part of "just" a teacher. *Self-description* becomes the baseline (standard) for what you will live up to; it is what you project to others and what you will receive from them in return. Those who say, "I'm just a . . ." get treated accordingly. Interestingly enough, those who say, "I am . . ." get treated with the respect they command. *You always get treated with the respect you command.*

Self-description becomes the baseline (standard) for what you will live up to.

Identity Windows: The Actual, Ideal, and Public Selves

The search for the answer to "Who Am I?" can be found in scrutinizing three distinct facets of your being — they are called the *actual*, *ideal*, and *public* windows. These self-perceptions form the basis for how *you* judge *who you are*.

The actual self is a composite picture of how successful you feel in each of your many roles as educator, friend, son, daughter, brother, sister, mother, father, painter, renter, owner and so on. You paint this picture based on your perception of how you're doing in each of these roles, *and* how you are greeted in each of them in return. For example, you may feel like a successful educator but not a very good parent if your child is not doing well academically, or you may feel good about your associations with friends but inadequate as a spouse if that relationship is not as nourishing as you would like it to be.

The ideal self is made up of your aspirations. It's the *ideal* of how you would like to be and who you want to become — the striving. "I wish I were more attractive, thinner, a better educator, an administrator, a business executive." It's the "if things were different" ideas and the belief in some day having or being those things.

The public self is the slice you are willing to show to others. It's the image you want these *others* to see. You can decide what this picture will be, or you can allow it to be influenced by what you think others want you to be (spirited, the faculty clown, the scapegoat). Miles Mitchell is noted among the faculty for being in a good mood at all times. His nickname is Miles O'Smiles because he always seems to have a happy grin on his face. He has come to accept being *always* happy as his role. Miles feels that he makes a positive contribution to his school by being cheerful, so he works hard at putting up a happy front even on the days when he's feeling down. As he explains, "Sometimes I get tired of having to live out this role, because I don't always feel it inside, but you know, everybody expects me to always be in a good mood, even when they aren't. Sometimes I just want to say, 'Hey, it's your turn. You cheer me up for a change.'" In this case, O'Smiles compromises his actual self for his public self. As can be detected in his analysis of his role, his reputation with himself pays a price.

What Does Your Picture Look Like?

It's important that your picture of yourself in each of these three areas be in perspective. When great discrepancies exist in the overall balance, the stress experienced can be enormous. When your life is mainly lived out projecting only the public self, for example, you can easily lose sight of how the other areas serve to keep you safe. This imbalance becomes magnified in the lives of famous people such as John Belushi. Belushi's public self was that of a clown and a slob, like the character he played in the film "Animal House." He put up the front of being a happy, exuberant guy, rather crass, uncaring, insensitive. The public was willing to accept him as such. They were less willing to accept him as a sensitive, romantic man. When Belushi tried to play a suave hero in the film "Continental Divide," he was a flop. The public had decided on the front it would accept and didn't respond well to any deviation from that.

A toll is exacted for having a life out of balance.

Belushi, like most of us, probably considered that he had more to offer than just a slapstick act. It must have been very difficult for him to know that the public refused to see more to the man than that front. No one would look past the humor to the intelligence and caring. Belushi's self-identity became more and more tied up in one self-window to the exclusion of others. A toll, whether in inappropriate behavior, drugs, depression, or anything else self-destructive, is exacted for having a life out of balance. The same can be said for the other windows; for example, a person is not his work role, yet some people define themselves solely by their working identity.

When a person has these three aspects of identity out of balance, he doesn't know who he is or what he stands for. He's in turmoil. Think of the superintendent who lives in a small town: If he acts primarily from his public self, he may think he has to always be dressed properly, perhaps even to shop at a local grocery store.

Gerry came from an upscale background, attended the best schools, and graduated near the top of his class. Now he is teaching at a top-quality prestigious prep school. He has been on the fast track all of his life and is feeling burned out. He loves teaching physical education to his high school students, but knows that everyone expects more of him. He "should" be working toward becoming the principal of the school, and then toward being a district-wide administrator. Gerry's friends tease him about being a "jock-maker," and are obviously expecting better things from him soon. In his own mind, Gerry, too, sees himself as going on to a higher position, but in his heart, he doesn't want the extra responsibility. His actual self, a very easy-going, relaxed sort of man, is in conflict with his ideal self who "should" be more successful. To complicate matters even further his actual self clashes with his public self. Gerry talks about the teaching position as "a stepping stone," further encouraging his friends to expect more of him. Gerry is in conflict on all three levels.

Building a Positive and Healthy Sense of Identity: An Inventory for Educators

Like the school bully who can learn to be a good guy, you, too, can change your self-description. Begin by assessing how *you see yourself* in each of these windows. Take some time to think about yourself in each of these areas. Then, using the following three questions, write out your descriptions.

- How would I describe my actual self?
- How would I describe my ideal self?
- How would I describe my public self?

This next assessment will help you gain a more in depth understanding and clarification of your identity. Begin by writing down as many words or phrases as you can to describe yourself in each of the following areas. Several examples are included as a way to get you thinking. Be as objective as possible, but don't be overly hard on yourself or put yourself down.

Like the school bully who can learn to be a good guy, you, too, can change your self-description.

SELF-CONCEPT INVENTORY

1. **My physical appearance:** Include descriptions of your height, weight, facial appearance, quality of skin, hair, style of dress, as well as descriptions of specific body areas such as your arms, chest, waist, neck, and legs.

   Example: 5'5"
   clear blue eyes
   large nose
   thick healthy hair
   too thin

2. **How I relate to others:** Include descriptions of your strengths and weaknesses in intimate relationships and in relationships to friends, family, co-workers, as well as how you relate to strangers in social settings.

   Example: socially competent
   not a very good listener
   warm
   accepting and flexible
   too accepting, then resentful

3. **How I would describe my personality:** Describe your positive and negative personality traits.

4. **How other people see me:** Describe the strengths and weaknesses that you think your friends, family, and co-workers see.

> **Example:** prompt
>
> hardworking
>
> disorganized
>
> motivated
>
> overstressed
>
> knowledgeable in the field
>
> restless
>
> not good at returning phone calls

Assess how well you reason and solve problems, your capacity for learning and creativity.

5. **Performance at work:** Include descriptions of the way you handle the major tasks at school.

> **Example:** efficient
>
> temperamental
>
> hard-driving

6. **Performance of the daily tasks of life:** Describe areas such as hygiene, health, maintenance of your living environment, food preparation, caring for your children, and any other ways you take care of personal or family needs.

7. **Mental functioning:** Include here an assessment of how well you reason and solve problems, your capacity for learning and creativity, general fund of knowledge, areas of special knowledge, wisdom you have acquired, insight and so on.

> **Example:** argumentative
>
> debate everything
>
> mentally lazy
>
> illogical
>
> intuitive
>
> quick-minded
>
> uncreative
>
> eager to learn new things
>
> curious about how things work

8. **My sexuality:** Describe how you see and feel about yourself as a sexual person.

When you are finished with the inventory, go back and put a plus sign by the items that represent strengths or things you like about yourself. Put a minus by items that you consider weaknesses or things you would like to change about yourself.

Example:

1. *Physical appearance*
   + 5'5"
   + clear blue eyes
   − large nose
   + thick healthy hair
   − too thin

2. *How I relate to others*
   + socially competent
   − not a very good listener
   + warm
   + accepting and flexible
   − too accepting, then resentful

4. *How others see me*
   + prompt
   + hardworking
   − disorganized
   + motivated
   − overstressed
   + knowledgeable in the field
   − restless
   − not good at returning phone calls

5. *Performance at work*
   + efficient
   − temperamental
   + hard-driving

7. *Mental functioning*
   − argumentative
   + debate everything
   − mentally lazy
   − illogical
   + intuitive
   + quick-minded
   − uncreative
   + eager to learn new things
   + curious about how things work

Self-esteem is somehow factored into the equation that determines the overall quality of one's life.

Listing Your Weaknesses

Now divide a clean sheet of paper into two columns. On the left side, write down each item you marked with a minus. Leave three lines between each item so that you'll have sufficient room to rewrite and make changes. Your goal is to rewrite the negatives, choosing instead to see the positive side of that area.

There's nothing wrong with having areas in which you don't like certain things about yourself. The problem lies in using weaknesses for destructive self-attacks. When rewriting your lists, there are four rules to keep in mind.

> **Rewrite the negatives, choosing instead to see the positive side of that area.**

1. **Use nonpejorative language.** Rather than say, "I am fat," say, "I am __ lbs. overweight." Go through your list and eliminate all words that have negative connotations.

2. **Use accurate language.** Don't exaggerate and don't embellish the negative. Revise the items on your list of weaknesses so that they are purely descriptive. Confine yourself to the facts.

3. **Use language that is specific rather than general.** Eliminate words like "everything," "always," "never," "completely," and so on. Rewrite the list so that your description is limited to the particular situation, setting, or relationship where the trait occurs. General indictments should be revised to reflect only the specific relationships where the problem occurs.

4. **Find exceptions or corresponding strengths.** This is an essential step for those items that really make you feel bad about yourself.

Revised Weaknesses List

Example:

   2. How I relate to others
   - + socially competent
   - − not a very good listener: *I listen to my students; I just don't listen to those colleagues I don't respect.*
   - + warm
   - + accepting and flexible
   - − too accepting, then resentful: *I let my sixteen-year-old son have his way but then I get resentful.*

   4. How others see me
   - + prompt
   - + hardworking
   - − disorganized: *I only do this when I am creating a new lesson plan for my special students.*

+   motivated
−   overstressed: *I'm usually tired and out of sorts when I get home. After I've taken some time to unwind, I'm revitalized.*
+   knowledgeable in the field
−   not good at returning phone calls: *I don't like returning phone calls prior to noon, but I don't mind returning them in the afternoon.*

Acknowledging Your Strengths

The next step is to acknowledge your strengths. You may have had experiences that make you reluctant to acknowledge your positive side, to give yourself credit for your assets. This is the time to acknowledge the things you appreciate about yourself. Go back to your Self-Concept Inventory. On a clean sheet of paper, write down all of the items marked with a plus. Read slowly down the items on your list of strengths. Try to think of other special qualities or abilities that you haven't mentioned. Think of compliments you've been given, note little successes, remember what you've overcome and what you've cared about. Include any awards or good marks you've earned. This exercise will help you to remember some of the things that you value about yourself.

To begin, think about the people you have most loved or admired. What makes you really like someone? On a piece of paper, write down those qualities that you have most appreciated in these individuals. Go over this list, using it as a tool for introspection. Go down the list slowly, item by item, and ask yourself which of these qualities applies to you. Look for examples from your past or present. You may be surprised that a number of the same qualities that inspire you to care for and respect others are descriptive of yourself as well. If any of the special qualities that you value in others and recognize in yourself have not been included in your list of strengths, add them now.

Go over your list one more time. Rewrite them in complete sentences, using synonyms, adjectives, and adverbs to elaborate. Get rid of negatives in favor of positives and eschew left-handed compliments. For example, rather than saying, "I am funny," say, "I have a quick, perceptive sense of humor that people really appreciate." Chances are you've been spending years dwelling on and polishing your list of negative qualities. Now give equal time to your strengths. Embellish the positive.

Give equal time to your strengths.

Creating a New Self-Description

It's time now to meld your strengths and weaknesses into a self-description that is accurate and supportive. This description will acknowledge weaknesses that you might change; it will also include the personal assets that are undeniably part of your identity. Your new description should cover all eight areas of the Self-Concept Inventory, including the more significant strengths and weaknesses (from the revised version only).

Read your new description out loud to yourself slowly and carefully, twice a day for four weeks. This is the minimum length of time for you to begin changing the ways you spontaneously think about yourself. Just as you learn a song by "getting the tune in your ear," you can learn more accurate ways of thinking about yourself by hearing your new self-description every day.

Most importantly, speak positively about yourself and others. When you speak positively about yourself, your colleagues, your school, your children at home, and your students, you impart the message that self-respect matters — your identity is to be valued.

THE IMPORTANCE OF YOUR APPEARANCE

Appearance counts. It's an unmistakable part of your identity. Whether you are acutely aware of it or not, a part of your self-concept has to do with how you *feel* about your appearance, and whether that is acceptable to you. Even the way you wear your hair and the physical shape you're in affects how you feel about yourself.

You can learn more accurate ways of thinking about yourself by hearing your new self-description every day.

Your mother may have said, "Beauty is only skin deep," but she wasn't talking about *your* perception of your attractiveness. The link between appearance and self-esteem begins at quite an early age. Children begin to form a concept of themselves (and others) based on "outer beauty," and to differentiate between what they consider to be "attractive and unattractive" at about three years of age. Children actually *stereotype* others on the basis of physical attractiveness. Attractive children are looked at, smiled at, touched, named as "best friends," and asked to play more often than other children.

Studies on the psychology of teaching reveal that teachers call on attractive children more often than unattractive children. Teachers define attractive as a generally neat and clean appearance. An attractive child has parents who have bothered to bathe and dress the child well, perhaps match a ribbon (or socks) to the child's attire. These children receive the most positive numbers of eye contacts by teachers and garner the most positive strokes (reinforcements) in the classroom as well. Such children receive a good share of positive attention, a plus in helping them cope with the normal frustrations of learning, and of course, in feeling good about themselves. Positive attention, stroking, touching, and verbal and nonverbal affirmations are the very factors that contribute to helping students become overachievers (or underachievers)! Don't keep this information from parents. They need to know how they "set the child up" for having (or not having) a good experience.

If you observe closely, you'll notice this criterion factored into the pecking order even in adulthood. Look closely and you'll notice that those who dress with a similar style often group themselves together. This is especially true in the business world where one of the "dress for success" connotations is played out in terms of who hangs out with whom (status), and can be a decisive factor in who will "advance" and when.

Dressing the Part

Many years ago when I began to feel burned out from teaching, I left the classroom and turned to the business sector. There I worked with a consulting company that held as one of its accounts Xerox Corporation. When I was given this account, I was initially surprised to find that "dress for success" had a different connotation than what we might normally think. As a part of my training for each corporate account, I was briefed as to what "uniform" was worn by the person I would be addressing. Whether I was calling on business executive A or B, it mattered that I find out the protocol of dress. It might be a standard pin-striped suit for dealing with the board of directors or senior management, or a soft silk dress for middle management — my appearance was to reflect that I had the savvy to gain entrance and assert status into the group. In this way, I could more readily gain acceptance so that I could get on with doing what I had come to do.

Just like one's mode of dress is important in gaining respect and acceptance in the business workplace, the importance of the "uniform" in the schoolplace cannot be underestimated. Those educators who appear to look like adults, rather than student look-alikes, generally are treated with more respect (from both students and colleagues) than fellow educators who try to blend in with their students. Those educators who look two decades behind the times are rarely valued as having relevant ideas or current information! Parents rarely view them as equals, let alone professionals, as they might value the opinion of a doctor for their child.

As a consultant with some 100 plus schools across the nation yearly, I can tell a lot about a school by viewing the faculty. Faculty members who look sharp generally are. Those who are still wearing polyester leisure suits are usually behind the times in terms of matching learning styles with teaching styles, in content area knowledge, in innovation in curriculum materials, and so on. A well-groomed and neat and clean appearance should be expected from staff and students. A general dress code ought to be in place in your setting. I visit faculties where you would be hard pressed to tell educators apart from their business counterparts. In other cases, I see educators that, judging by their appearance, look like they care very little about themselves or their roles. What you look like matters in terms of your influence and power, not only with each other, but with your clients, your students.

How would you rate your appearance? Take a moment to conduct a quick inventory. Ask yourself these questions:

- When was the last time I took stock of my appearance?
- How does my overall appearance compare to that of my colleagues?
- Am I clean and well groomed each day?
- Am I over/underdressed?
- How do I feel about my appearance?
- How would my students describe my appearance?
- How would my peers describe my appearance?

> **What you look like matters in terms of your influence and power.**

- How would the parents of my students describe my appearance?
- How does looking sharp affect the way I feel about myself on a given day?
- What is the effect of my appearance on my self-esteem?

Looking the part doesn't have to mean a big emphasis on clothes, but rather, that you are neat and clean and feel good about your appearance. Demonstrating pizzazz doesn't hurt either!

ASSERTING YOURSELF

A healthy identity allows you to stand up for yourself, to be who you are openly — in a word, assertive. To be assertive means to value yourself — to act with confidence and authority. Assertion is "owning" what you need and not putting the responsibility on someone else. Assertion is communicating in a manner that is direct, self-respecting, and straightforward without causing anyone else duress.

People respect honesty, even criticism if it's presented in an open, honest and respectful way. Statements that affirm what you are feeling and what you need represent a way of taking responsibility for and respecting yourself, of asserting your needs and wants.

To be assertive means to value yourself — to act with confidence and authority.

Assessing Your Assertiveness

How good are you at communicating your needs? Do you let others know how you're feeling? Here are some questions to check your ability to stand your ground.

- The school coach cuts in the lunch line, ignoring the feelings of others. "I've got to get to practice," he says without looking at anyone in particular. What do you say?
- A colleague teaching the same course you are asks to use the test you've prepared for your students. You don't feel like handing it over. What do you say?
- The teacher next door keeps her entire class after school because someone was talking against the rules. Several of those students need to catch the bus for a football game at a nearby school. What do you do (you are the coach)?
- What can you do if another teacher is in the habit of ridiculing students in the teacher's lounge?
- You don't understand a new school policy. What would you say in asking for help?
- A school board member's daughter isn't doing so well in your class. You are a new teacher to the district, still on your probationary period. What do you do?

■ One of your fellow teachers has a reputation as a poor teacher. What do you do and/or say?

■ You agree to meet a friend after school for a social visit, but then realize you have a ton of papers that need to be handed back to students tomorrow. What do you do? What do you say to your friend when you see him?

■ You shared an idea of yours with a colleague who brings it up at a faculty meeting and doesn't mention that it's your idea. Even though it's a small point, it bothers you. How do you react?

■ Your principal makes a point of praising other teachers when talking to you, but rarely mentions anything you have done well. You're becoming irritated at hearing their praises sung while nothing is said about your hard work. Do you say anything to the principal, and if so, what?

Questions like these cover situations you have probably encountered in your daily work. The goal is to make you think about how you handle them, what you say, how you react. Your reactions say a lot about the type of person you consider yourself to be. If you are not happy with your lack of assertiveness, do a little role-playing when you're alone or with friends. Put yourself in each situation and work through it. It's much easier to be assertive when you're prepared.

Your reactions say a lot about the type of person you consider yourself to be.

DISCUSSION: A Lesson Plan for Educators

1. What are the actual, ideal, and public selves? How can we identify them? Is it normal to have disparity between them? How much disparity is normal? In other words, how big of a gap does there have to be before we become concerned?

2. How important is appearance to one's self-esteem? Should we as adults give the same weight to it that our students do? How can we look beyond appearance, overcome first impressions? What does your own appearance say about you?

3. How can we find out what the perception is of our public selves? How can we relate appearance to our ideal selves?

4. What is the difference between assertiveness and aggression? How can we identify our level of assertiveness; what are the key factors to look for? What level of assertiveness is appropriate for the educator? Is it possible for a passive, generally laid-back person to increase her level of assertiveness, or will that cause stress by being contrary to her natural personality?

Chapter 9

AFFILIATION:
The Need for Bonding and Group Membership

A Feeling of Belonging Increases Self-Esteem

Affiliation is the deep-seated desire to be with others, to be accepted, to belong. Most of us seek to be accepted by others, particularly by those whom we consider to be important to us. Whether you term this need for belonging, *bonding, synergy,* or *socialization* — and call those who become a part of those you need *friends, peers, colleagues,* or *team-players* — wanting *connection* is a normal human need. Knowing that others *accept* us adds self-value. And when our self-esteem is healthy, we're more likely to value and accept others in return.

Though most everyone needs to feel connected to others in some way, not everyone *feels* that they belong. That's what loneliness, and at its extreme — suicide — is about. Not to be wanted, needed, or valued by others (and most especially ourselves) saddens us, lowering our self-esteem. Feelings of isolation and alienation are painful. We need only look to the increasing numbers of *planned* pregnancies, suicides, and school dropouts to see how devastating feeling disconnected can be to young adults:

- **Pregnancy.** Of the more than one million adolescent girls who became pregnant last year, nearly 85% said they believed that having a baby would provide them with the love and acceptance that their parents and teachers did not. Many said they wanted a baby because it would give them "someone to love."

- **Suicide.** Suicide statistics have gone up 300% each year in the past five years, reaching into younger and younger youth populations.

- **Dropouts.** More and more (and younger and younger) youth are leaving school. Studies from the Center for Educational Statistics on school dropouts clearly substantiate that a feeling of being "unaffiliated" — of not belonging — is the second leading cause of leaving school before graduation.

> When our self-esteem is healthy, we're more likely to value and accept others in return.

People who do not feel they belong are more likely to:

- have difficulty making and keeping friendships
- be easily influenced by others
- be low achievers
- be uncomfortable working in group settings
- isolate themselves from others and become even more lonely
- assert themselves by being uncooperative or ridiculing others
- experience mental health problems

In contrast, those with a sense of belonging are more able to:

- initiate friendships
- show sensitivity toward others
- cooperate and share with others
- achieve acceptance easily and be sought out by others
- feel valued by others
- express happiness
- excel in their work

Educators Need to Feel a Part of the Team

Feeling acceptance — connection — contributes to a positive sense of self. Educators who have developed good relationships with friends and peers, and who have strong family ties have a higher self-esteem than those who do not.

Not all educators feel connected to their profession. Though teachers have an illusion of being a part of a "school," the nature of their work more often than not leads to isolation. That many educators yearn for a greater sense of community with their colleagues, their students, and with other professionals within the district is no surprise. I've been in schools where it's impossible for the educator to spend more than five to six minutes each day with anyone other than their students. The schedule and subject matter may be such that the educator even ends up eating lunch in his room alone.

There's no question about the benefits of a positive sense of community. Those who do feel a sense of community are more likely to describe the nature of their work in positive terms, seek feedback from their colleagues, and openly participate in a range of educational activities. They are also more likely to show an interest and openness to the ideas of their colleagues, and a receptiveness to the needs of their students. Such responsiveness not only nourishes their colleagues'

That many educators yearn for a greater sense of community . . . is no surprise.

sense of self, but forms the basis for mutually fortifying relationships that contribute to their own self-esteem.

How about you? Do you feel you get your membership needs met in a satisfying and nourishing way? Do you have all the acceptance you want and need from your colleagues, administrators, students and parents? If not, what can you do? Here are some suggestions. Again, add your own. Talk these out with your faculty.

Do You "Belong?" Increasing Your Membership Skills

1. Show acceptance. Caring and acceptance are vital to helping colleagues feel connected to you. Here are some ways you can show acceptance:

- **Verbal expressions.** Express acceptance. Say the words directly — don't simply hint at them. Make remarks such as: "You've been so helpful to me on this project, Robert," "I really like team-teaching with you, Mary," "I really like being a part of this staff," or "I really do want to get more involved." From these remarks, your colleagues draw conclusions about how you accept them, and *how much you want to be connected to them.*

- **Empathic listening.** A good listener builds a relationship and sets the foundation for mutual caring. When you take the time to listen, you're telling the other person that he or she is valuable and worthy of your time and attention. Listening is about understanding: It helps the other person feel valued. The next time a colleague wants to talk about something important to him, observe your listening style. Are you fidgeting and looking restless, or are you showing interest in what he has to say? Look at him, meeting his eyes. Give him your complete attention. Imagine how you would feel if you went to another teacher's room, bursting with big news. You launch into the whole story, but it's obvious your colleague is bored and his attention is wandering. How do you feel? You feel deflated. And you're an adult, aware of your feelings, able to isolate the action (the lack of attentiveness) from the intent — obviously your colleague never meant to hurt your feelings or disparage your accomplishment. To the other person, you merely stopped listening. That means that they're not as important to you, and that maybe their accomplishment wasn't such a big deal after all. They feel a little less valued.

> When you take the time to listen, you're telling the other person that he or she is valuable.

Listening expresses the attitude of "I want to understand you." When you listen, you make it clear that you care about your colleague's interests, concerns, needs, hopes, fears, doubts, and joys. *Listening is really a matter of acceptance.* It's accepting another person's ideas and feelings, and being okay about the fact that this other viewpoint may be different than yours. Know that *from every person's point of view, he is right.* You say in a cheerful tone, "Good, you see it differently. I would like to understand how you see it." This conveys, "I see it differently," rather than, "I'm right and you're wrong." Such language admits, "Like mine, your views and feelings are legitimate and respectable. You matter to me, I want to understand you." Do you show, by listening, that you value your colleagues?

■ **"WE" language.** Get in the habit of using language that shows group membership. Words like *our, we,* and *us* show desire for inclusion. Use group membership language in the classroom as well. In the teachers' lounge, you probably brag about "my students." It's important to you to feel connected to your colleagues. It's just as important for your colleagues to have a sense of affiliation with you. Your words and actions of acceptance reflect your willingness to allow others access to you.

2. Expand your network. You may need to expand your circle of associations or enrich the ones to which you belong. There are many ways in which you can. For example, by joining a social organization, sports club, or church group, you can broaden your range of interests and activities. Make a list of all the groups, clubs, associations, and networks available to you in meeting your needs for membership. Don't forget about subscribing to professional magazines. This can help you feel that you belong to a bigger educational community.

3. Cultivate professional support systems. Having a base of peer support is an important part of feeling like you belong. Raising a family and putting in long hours at work can make you feel as if you rarely spend time with colleagues, and can give the illusion that you have developed fewer friendships than is actually the case. Getting together with colleagues to share feelings, ideas and strategies can be as therapeutic as it is networking, and can help you feel connected. A support system reduces your feelings of alienation, empowers and refuels self-esteem, and provides comradery — the insulation that can prevent burnout.

A support system reduces your feelings of alienation.

Who are all the members of your professional support system? Using the example below, take the time to identify all of them:

Name: _____

What this person does to demonstrate support: _____

_____

4. Cultivate a support system outside of teaching. Aside from your professional support group, there are other people who can provide you with a sense of connection, provide objectivity, reassurance, fun and warmth, and additional perspective. I'm fond of the expression, "There are glass balls and rubber balls in life. The goal is to know which is which. *Family, health, and friends are the glass balls. You must NEVER drop the glass balls."*

Using the example below, take the time now to list the people who provide you support, friendship, and nourishment.

Name: _____

What this person does to demonstrate support: _____

_____

5. Be proactive on relationship-building. We tell our students that in order to *have* a friend, you have to *be* a friend. That's good advice for us too. Have you noticed how some teachers seem to quietly and unassumingly command attention and admiration from their students and colleagues, while other teachers "can get no respect"? Good teachers have learned the importance of establishing rapport with their students and understand its contribution to bringing students to the learning experience. These educators also take the time to nurture support from their colleagues for their own sense of satisfaction and for the benefit of meeting the educational goals of the school.

Building relationships is a matter of caring. When others sense you care, they are secure, validated and affirmed of their intrinsic worth. You make it easy for them to respect you and want to cooperate with you. You have positively influenced them. One of the most important relationship-building skills is that of the emotional bank account.

The Emotional Bank Account

With each person in your life you open an *emotional bank account*. The concept works just like your account at the bank. What you do and say can be a deposit or a withdrawal in the emotional account. Deposits are made through positive and helpful actions — courtesy, respect, kindness, honesty, dependability, constancy, fairness, and professional effectiveness. Withdrawals are made through discourtesy, disrespect, put-downs, emotional distance, poor quality teaching, papers poorly marked, and so on. I'm a parent of a sixteen-year-old. Here's how this principle works for me:

What you do and say can be a deposit or a withdrawal in the emotional account.

My daughter Jennifer's curfew is 11:00. When I ask that she honor her curfew and be in by that time, I mean for her to be in by 11:00. It's negotiable only in a few special cases. Mandate or not, should she choose to violate it, she could. That's out of my control and completely up to her. How will I get her to honor the curfew, or in unforeseeable circumstances, call immediately to explain her plight?

The best way is to have her *want* to uphold the curfew because she, too, values our relationship and doesn't want to break the trust she has with me. In other words, I better have a good relationship with her, and more specifically, I should have a "positive balance" in our account, in order for her to value the time commitment (curfew). If I have a negative balance in the emotional bank account with my daughter — if I'm in the habit of making promises but not keeping them, for example, or treating her unfairly, then because she is upset, and rightly so, she may very well do a "withdrawal" on my emotional account. By not being in on time, or by not calling, she knows she can cause me worry and anguish. On the other hand, if I keep making deposits in our emotional bank account, my reserves build up. Her trust in me becomes greater, and I can call on that trust if I need to. I can even make a few minor mistakes, causing withdrawals, and still be forgiven.

But if I continually make withdrawals from the account without making deposits, the reserve is diminished. If I keep making withdrawals, the emotional bank account becomes overdrawn. At that point I have little, if any, trust with her. I have to watch every step.

Darlene Hutchinson is an elementary school principal. She is liked and respected by staff, students, and parents. She is also well-respected in the district. Darlene is a good school manager. Her greatest successes have come not only from the way she manages the school as an organization, but from the relationship building she has done with staff, students, and parents. Darlene is visible — in the halls mingling with students and faculty — and is known for her effective style in communicating with parents. Says Darlene, "The most important time I spend is with people. That has more payoff than all the rules, policies, and training I could possibly put in place."

Gene is a high school Spanish teacher. His peers have learned that Gene, while a good teacher, is quite uninterested in being a synergistic part of the faculty. When assigned a role in a faculty project, for example, he will procrastinate, and then do a slapdash job at the very end. For this reason, his peers have little confidence in him. They rarely count on him to attend a social gathering at their homes, and they assign him minuscule roles in projects the entire faculty is expected to participate in. In short, they don't trust that he will be a team player. Gene senses that something is wrong; he knows he doesn't fit in, but can't understand why. "I work as hard as any teacher here," he says, "but no one appreciates me." Gene doesn't have a sense of affiliation. His emotional bank account is always in the red.

Emotional bank accounts are very fragile.

Emotional Bank Accounts Are Fragile, but Resilient

Emotional bank accounts are very fragile, but at the same time, very resilient. If I have a large emotional bank account, say an imaginary sum of $1,000 of emotional reserve capacity with my daughter, I can make small withdrawals of $10 from time to time and she will understand and overlook it. For instance, I may need to make a very unpopular, authoritarian decision without even involving her. Let's say that Jennifer wants to attend a three-day camping trip and I'm not feeling comfortable with how the activity will be chaperoned. I may say, "No. You can't go. I will not support this particular activity." She may pout or be very angered, and she'll tell me so. My unpopular decision may cost me $100 in her eyes. But if I have a $1,000 bank account and I make a $100 withdrawal, I will still have $900 left. In other words, it's unlikely that she will go to her room, pack for the trip, and go anyway! (Though that is always an option!)

I can also try to lessen the amount of the withdrawal. For example, I can explain why I don't want her to go, giving her my reasoning and so on, thus possibly redepositing some portion of the $100. In addition, I can work out other ways to "raise the cash to remove the negative withdrawal" — perhaps I can suggest that she call up a favorite friend and invite her over for a special weekend. I may offer to pay for the movie rather than keeping with my current rule that she use her allowance money for such activities. I may pay for special theater tickets, or allow a curfew later than usual, just to show my willingness to be compassionate about the fact that she isn't where she wants to be. Therefore, I may even get back twenty or thirty "emotional dollars," or some portion of the original withdrawal.

Do You Have a Positive (or Negative) Balance in Your "Account?"

Like my influence with my daughter, and Darlene's influence with her staff, students and their parents, and Gene with his colleagues, your influence with students and colleagues depends upon your relationship with each one. When withdrawals exceed deposits, the account is overdrawn. If you threaten, ignore, ridicule, put-down, or if you are unfair, harsh, or unreasonable, relationships will deteriorate. A lack of deposits leads to an overdrawn emotional bank account, a breakdown of the relationship, and a lack of influence. In short, you have a problem on your hands, and you have contributed to it.

Make every effort to provide your colleagues (and your students) with encouragement and praise.

Given that the emotional "bank account" is so important in the overall scheme of things, what can you do to build up your account? Making daily *deposits* yields the best dividends. While only you know what works best with each person in your life, these are the basics:

- **Don't talk negatively (about your students or other teachers.)** Most people live up to your expectations. To demonstrate your willingness to believe in the goodness of another person can be a huge deposit — which can lead to others wanting to prove themselves worthy of your trust.

- **Respect your students and colleagues.** If you want respect, you have to give it. People resent you for not treating them with dignity and respect. You have to give respect in order to gain respect.

- **Give encouragement and praise.** Make every effort to provide your colleagues (and your students) with encouragement and praise. Of course, your comments should be sincere and your praise deserved, or they'll mean little and render your credibility shallow at best.

- **Sincerely apologize when you are wrong.** You make a deposit when you can sincerely say: "I was wrong," "I'm sorry." People are very forgiving when you acknowledge that you have been unfair. If you embarrass a colleague in front of his peers, acknowledge it. Say, "John, I'm afraid I took the credit for your idea at the faculty meeting today. I'm sorry. That was unfair." Such recognition not only reduces the amount of the withdrawal but becomes a deposit. But there's a limit. *You can't talk your way out of something you've behaved your way into.* Apologies lose their meaning when you keep repeating your transgressions.

6. Build a sense of community within your faculty. Educators, like all professionals, need a sense of comradery, the feeling that "we're all in this together." With the sad lack of respect that our profession has in many quarters these days, we need to support one another, to validate our career choice, to applaud one another for gains made, to reassure each other that we are in fact making a difference — when we are. We need to build a sense of community.

A sense of community helps us feel like we belong — so critical to self-esteem. Community is built by sharing, by communicating thoughts and ideas and experiences. Show that you value being part of the group, that you respect your colleagues' opinions and input, that they are a significant part of the reason you enjoy your job as much as you do. The things you do to show your colleagues that you know what's going on increases their feelings of being valued. Here are some ways to make your peers feel *special*.

> **Community is built by sharing, by communicating thoughts and ideas and experiences.**

- **Tell them.** "I enjoy your friendship so much, John," "I can always count on you, Michael," or "You guys make me glad I belong to this faculty."

- **Talk about why you're happy to be a part of the "team."** Don't give your colleagues the feeling that teaching is a chore and this faculty is a burden to be endured. Don't make them feel like they are a bunch of behavior misfits, or that you're stuck with them. You want them to feel special and worthy. Individual members will respond to your attitudes about them.

- **Be encouraging.** One important educational philosophy is that all students can learn. In getting each student to learn, especially the low self-esteem and reluctant learner, you need to help the student to see his successes so that he will be encouraged to tackle bigger challenges. In order for a student to succeed, he must first believe he can. Likewise, the educator wonders if his hard work and effort are paying off. When you sense that a colleague is having a tough day, be the first to remind this faculty member of his or her previous successes. Be encouraging. Just like learning is tough work, teaching is too.

- **Offer friendship.** Are you a friendly faculty member? Do others value your friendship? If you aren't satisfied with what you find, work to change it. How about colleagues? Look around. How many educators seem to be "friendless?"

- **Communicate community.** In an environment where a sense of community exists, people feel valuable and worthy. It takes time and effort to understand others, and sometimes you feel you don't have all day to sit and listen. But in fact, it takes far more time to deal with misunderstandings and hard feelings. When you take the time to listen, you have communicated many things: you want to understand; you care; you respect the other person's feelings; you value his or her friendship; and you value the relationship. Just as they teach for cooperative learning, educators need to bring about a synergistic work environment among themselves.

DISCUSSION: A Lesson Plan for Educators

1. Is belonging as important to adult professionals as it is to students? Do we outgrow our need for affiliation? How does your school staff measure up in terms of being supportive to each other?

2. How can you tell whether you are accepted and valued by your colleagues? What steps can you take to increase your belonging? How can you identify what things you are doing that lower your group memberships; what do you do to alienate others? How can you change that and gain acceptance?

3. How can we create a sense of belonging if the faculty has always been very independent, not functioning as a team? Are educators more or less likely to work together than other professionals, and how can we take advantage of that or work around it?

Chapter 10

COMPETENCE:
Are You a "Can-Do" Person?

The Power to Turn Negatives Into Positives

A fifth element of self-esteem is competence — a sense of being capable. Being capable, having mastery, is an *empowering* feeling, lending itself to self-confidence, which in turn stimulates your efforts, leading to achievement, and feeding into successes. It's a sustaining and repeating cycle, or as the saying goes, "Success stimulates success." You soon have a storehouse of positive reminders of being a capable person.

Seeing yourself as a "can-do" person will serve you well in many ways. When faced with an obstacle you'll generate alternatives. When you do poorly at something, you'll discount its negative value, put it behind you, and move on. Because you erase it from the error column, the outcome is a positive growth experience rather than a debilitating one.

Seeing yourself as a "can-do" person will serve you well in many ways.

The Ten Characteristics of Highly Satisfied People

This attitudinal "skill" is central to doing well in life, as Gail Sheehy's findings reveal in her excellent book, *Pathfinders*. Sheehy wanted to know why — when met with crisis — some people were defeated by the trauma, while others found creative ways to remove the obstacle, jump the hurdles, and continue on their way. Sheehy's research reveals ten characteristics of such people. Each was able to say:

■ My life has meaning and direction.
■ I have experienced one or more important transitions in my life and have handled these in a positive way.
■ I rarely feel cheated or disappointed by life.
■ I have attained several long-term goals that are important to me.
■ Personal growth and development are important and ongoing for me.
■ I have mutually loving relationships in my life.
■ I have many friends.
■ I am a cheerful person.
■ I am not crushed by criticism.
■ I have no major fears.

Of those ten qualities, one very important point stood out. *Highly satisfied adults said they rarely felt disappointed or cheated by life, **because** they were able to learn from their experiences.* Nearly everyone of these individuals had failed at something major, but all had recast the experience in their minds. They had erased the outcome from the error column and had come to see the experience as a plus. "What I learned from that experience . . ." was a common statement made by all. The so-called "bad experience" was found to be a useful one, so much so that they rated it near the top of those events they said contributed to their "success."

The so-called "bad experience" was found to be a useful one.

Exactly the opposite was the case with low self-esteem people, who described their crisis as a personal failure and a destructive experience, and saw themselves as victims instead of being in charge. These individuals did not see themselves as capable of transforming the experience into one that would allow them to go forward with their lives. The experience had cast doubts on their capabilities, and they became fearful, cynical, and overwhelmed by their fate. Many were very angry that life had dealt them such a fatal blow. Few saw how they themselves had engineered their own fate, and even fewer took responsibility for what had happened. Unwilling to pick up the pieces and go forward, many had actually dropped out of the workforce, abandoned their spouse or children, allowed their health to deteriorate, and started coping through a cycle of chemical or substance abuse.

How Attitude Affects Performance

"You can if you think you can." "It's mind over matter." "There's nothing you can't do if you put your mind to it." How many times have you made these or similar statements to your students? How often have you told a discouraged child that he could be successful if he tried, again?

Attitude is one of the critical determinants of performance. When you believe that your career is important, when you feel that what you are doing is enriching lives, when your attitude about yourself and your job is positive, you are more likely to strive for first-rate competence in your work. Having a good attitude doesn't mean that you will automatically succeed at everything you do, but it does make it more likely that you will. Notice the outcomes associated with a person who feels capable.

A person who feels capable:

• is eager to do things, to achieve
• is willing to self-correct when he meets with failure
• accepts challenges
• uses mistakes as learning tools

- knows his strengths and leads with them
- displays good sportsmanship even in the face of failure
- has effective strategies for handling defeat
- recognizes accomplishments and achievements as important to growth
- gives himself positive self-statements and encouragement

Compare this to a person with low self-esteem and you'll see just the opposite. The person magnifies his weaknesses and failures. Having experienced too few successes and frequent failures, he's reluctant to try again. The attitude of "Why try, I'm just going to lose again anyway" begins a self-defeating pattern. He believes his unsuccessful experience is a sign of personal failure and inadequacy. The message he gives himself is, "I won't be able to do it. I can't do it." Not feeling capable, he acts helpless. He is unwilling to take risks, has an overriding fear of failure, and is a poor loser. He uses negative self-statements ("I'm so dumb") and discounts or discredits his achievements ("I was just lucky"). How can such traits possibly lead to experiencing achievement and success?

Competence and self-esteem fuel each other: Feeling capable enhances our sense of self; the level of our self-esteem, in turn, contributes to the goals we set and achieve.

You need to know how you affect the learning experience.

It's Imperative That Educators Feel Capable

Like any professional doing his or her job well, as an educator you must be a very capable person. You need to know what it's like to be a child tackling the challenges associated with learning and coping in the schoolplace. You need to know how *you* affect the learning experience, you need to know about teaching and learning outcomes — how students best learn, how your own nature bears out in the instructional role. You must know about your content area, of course, and you must know what to ask of parents in supporting their child as a learner. Teaching is a big job with big-time responsibilities — definitely not for the shy of heart! Let's examine one of the most important roles — knowing your clients.

ARE YOU AN EXPERT ON YOUR CLIENTS (STUDENTS)?

Educators are in the business of developing human potential. *Actually it's not so much that educators develop potential, but that they help youth become aware that their capacity for being and doing is infinite and, here's the catch, that they hold the key to discovering and unfolding that rich vastness of possibilities.* In doing so, educators ought first to know something about what humans have a capacity for — both in the area of being and doing. Research in the last ten years has produced a wealth of information about how humans unfold — how they learn and change, unfold and develop. As an educator you must possess this information, not only for your own feelings of teaching competence, but in order to work effectively with children.

The more you know about the psychology of children at each age in the childhood years — what it's like being two or five, six or nine, eleven or seventeen — the more you learn about the nature of childhood, and about the limitations and expansiveness of each year of life. For example, research shows that children are more vulnerable at certain ages to specific fears and anxieties than at others. A child's primary need at fourteen is for *unconditional acceptance* of himself as an individual. He wants to be accepted, no matter what. Long hair, green hair, or shaved hair, his actions will center on gaining approval and total acceptance for his individual sense of self. This necessary and natural developmental stage is called *"(seeking) autonomy."* This differs from a five-year-old, whose primary need is to be *with* his parents, preferably all the time; he pines for and worries about them when he is away from them. He'd like to spend the daytime hours with his parents and sleep in their room at night! Being without his parents, his greatest fear, causes him great distress. We call this necessary and natural developmental stage *"separation anxiety."* Whereas the fourteen-year-old seeks separation from his parents, the five-year-old is debilitated by it.

> **The particular stage of development a student is experiencing is one of the driving motivations as reflected in his behavior.**

The particular stage of development a student is experiencing is one of the driving factors behind his motivations as reflected in his behavior. By being aware of these developmental stages, you can better understand the work that a child must undertake at each stage (and consequently, his behavior), and thus help him learn acceptable ways to respond to the challenges, people, and events in his life. This awareness also enables you to develop a curriculum around an area of need and so achieve the best result in this student's learning.

A Crash Course in Child Development: Stages and Their Tasks

If you listen closely, you will learn that most educators have a preference for working with one age of students over another. This is because each stage of a child's development presents its own set of tasks and demands, all focused on gaining self-knowledge — **selfhood.** We say, "A child's play is his work." A child's work at each stage is pretty well defined. Though it's not possible to go through each age of a child's life in detail here, I'll give you a general overview. The suggested reading section at the back of this book provides additional resources, and you may wish to consult your district's child development specialists (or psychologists, school nurse or counselor) for further information in gaining a more comprehensive picture of childhood and developmental tasks, especially as it relates to the age and grade level you teach.

Age Two: Autonomy. Up until the age of two a child primarily views himself as part of his mother (or father, if he is the primary caretaker). Upon reaching two, he becomes aware that he is, in reality, separate from her. This presents him with the task of establishing autonomy — separateness. The two words that best describe his newfound selfhood, that he is in fact a separate person, are "NO" and "MINE!" Possession is a tool he uses to enforce that sense of a separate self.

Implications for Developing Self-Esteem: Parents who have experienced their child's zealous work on this task of *selfness* without understanding it have no doubt at one time or another said, "He's reached the Terrible Two's." But the two-year-old is neither a selfish nor an obstinate child. He's looking for power and ways to assert it. Assisting this child's developing sense of self is a matter of allowing him power and ways to be (safely) assertive. This child needs to be given choices.   For example, he can pick out which shoes he wants to wear or what toy he wants to play with. He can decide which book he wants to have read to him. In each instance, the child can be provided with two or three choices, all of which a parent can live with.

The autonomy the young child develops at this stage lays the foundation for being able to value himself. Through his "work" he learns that he can assert himself — the forerunner of independence. If the developmental tasks of being two have been met with a fair degree of success, at age three he will be quite independent.

> Through his "work" he learns that he can assert himself.

Age Three: Mastery. Having realized his separateness, the three-year-old goes on to master his environment. Mastery plays an important role in his perception of self: It influences his feeling of being capable (or not capable). His need for *success* in his endeavors at this stage is crucial. He labors over each of his accomplishments. Because he is slow and methodical, it takes him forever to do each task! Needing feedback to know if he has been successful, he strives for *recognition* of these achievements. ("Watch me! Watch me!") That he has something to offer nurtures his sense of competence and proves his value — he is worthwhile.

The search for mastery stimulates curiosity. "Why, why, why?" she wants to know. Her *drive* for discovering (learning) is insatiable — her *capacity* for learning is unlimited. It's not uncommon for her to hum continuously or sing her thoughts — it helps her concentrate, to stay with the moment, because the mind is moving so fast. She has an incredible ease in learning languages and language-related skills. With vigor she explores her surroundings, observes people, and examines how she fits into each relationship — this and more.

Implications for Developing Self-Esteem: Parents need patience to answer this child's repeated questions. She is exploring her environment, examining everything closely. Her achievements should be recognized with much praise and tangible signs such as putting her drawings up where they are visible. Parents and day-care workers can show they have in fact listened to her by asking her to tell them about something she enjoys discussing, such as how or why she has drawn a certain picture, or why she has chosen to use certain colors in the picture.

Age Four: Initiative. The four-year-old's task is developing *self-initiative* — the forerunner of self-responsibility. This may involve something as simple as taking responsibility for putting his toys away after he's done playing with them, as detailed as making his own bed — complete with lumps and crooked sheets, lumpy covers and corners — or as complex as learning to tie his shoelaces. What's most important to him is that he took it upon himself to do it — to attempt it, to strive for it..

Implications for Developing Self-Esteem: This child's *attempts* should be commended and allowed, whenever possible, to remain exactly as completed by him. Praise should be focused not on the *way* the task was done, but on the fact that it was *attempted* and/or *completed*. To improve the way he does a particular task, he should be shown rather than told what to do. Experience, not words, is his best teacher now. This will encourage further displays of his initiative, while also encouraging self-confidence.

Age Five: Separation Anxiety. Parents are the name of the game for the five-year-old. At this age, the mother is the center of the child's world. He not only wants to please her, he wants to be near her, talk with her, play with her, go to work with her, help her around the house, or go along on errands, and he would prefer to be with her than with friends. This does not mean that the father is left out of the picture. While the mother is the preferred, the father is definitely important too.

The five-year-old's adoration of his parents is unquestionably heartwarming. The result is almost totally parent-pleasing behavior. The good news for the educator is that since children transfer their feelings of respect for their parents onto the teacher, teachers at this stage are adored and loved. (Ever notice how kindergarten teachers long to stay in their assignment for decades and rarely burn out?) The child's basic framework is, "I want to be good all the time. I want to not do any of the bad things; I'll do whatever you say." Not only does he want and mean to be good, but he more often than not succeeds in being good. In his determination to do everything just right, he'll ask permission for even the simplest thing, even when he needn't, and he will then beam with pleasure when you smile and give permission. (Later on in this chapter I'll be using this age to illustrate how a child's developmental needs can be factored into curriculum development.)

> He is a person in his own right — "separate" feelings are all right.

Implications for Developing Self-Esteem: Most important in this period is helping the student recognize that he is a person in his own right, that "separate" feelings are all right. Especially important is allowing this student the feeling of being good, doing right, and winning your approval. Because separation anxiety is very real to him, reassure him of his parents' safety.

Age Six: MEness. "Self-centeredness" comes before "other-centeredness." While at the preschool stage this child discovered he was separate from his parents, he still kept his parents at the center of his existence. At six, he must shift his focus from his parents to himself: He now places himself at the center of his world rather than parents or others. Though he appears to be self-centered, this is an important milestone in his development. He is now ready to undertake the task of being receptive to his own interests as he attempts to understand them.

Implications for Developing Self-Esteem: Allow this age of student reasonable room to make some of his own decisions. This doesn't mean you let him have everything he wants; it means that you show acceptance while simultaneously setting boundaries and healthy limits. Strive to build his individual sense of self by designing projects that invite his discovering a wide variety of interests. When you see a particular area of interest, allow him to delve into it. Present him with several options for doing things, again, all of the options being those you can live with. For example, he may sit where he would like, or sharpen his pencil without permission (provided he doesn't create a disturbance). Be tolerant with his boasting, but keep comparisons with other peers — whether schoolwork or playtime activities — to a minimum.

Ages Seven to Eight: Sameness. Having established a "me," he moves on to the next stage. Now the need to be separate takes a back seat to his need to feel "oneness" with his same-age, same-sex peers. As he makes the move from self to others, playmates are the new "reflectors," and friends become more important. Mastery of social and physical skills becomes the common language to gauge how well he's doing with them.

Implications for Developing Self-Esteem: Students should be encouraged to join same-age groups, provided with opportunities to develop skills in a variety of activities, and helped to learn healthy and positive ways to relate to others — namely, acquiring and maintaining friendships. Teach and reinforce the skills of fairness and cooperation.

Ages Nine to Ten: Sitting on the Fence. Duality of needs exists for this child — he needs approval, direction, and affirmation from *both* adults and peers. At this stage the continued need to be with members of the same sex is a matter of developing sexual identity. Though outwardly this child may claim and exhibit contempt for the opposite sex, very often she has a secret boyfriend, he a secret girlfriend. Games of boys chasing girls or vice versa are common. This behavior is normal and is part of this task of forming sexual identity — necessary in becoming heterosexual. His task is to learn ways of being masculine, hers, ways of being feminine. He also tries to get a feel for how males and females behave by imitating the same-sex parent. Because he repeats what he hears others say, his comments often seem off the wall to the task at hand. He is busy thinking out loud.

His task is to learn ways of being masculine, hers, ways of being feminine.

Implications for Developing Self-Esteem: This is a good age to teach students to perform little courtesies, such as holding out a coat for someone to shrug into or opening a door. It's at this stage that boys in particular need to learn the difference between being strong and being rough; emphasize the importance of not hurting anyone with their strength (that this child is often rough and hurtful to pets or other small animals involves a show of dominance that must be discouraged). Girls need to learn the difference between being feminine and being weak. Learning about people is the focus: This is the age to introduce books on relationships that give students a sense of caring for and valuing others. It's a good time to study cultures other than their own and, generally, assume a social consciousness.

Ages Eleven to Twelve: Regrouping and Taking Stock. This is a comparatively mellow time, placed between two major periods of intense growth. It's a time for refining physical and academic competence as well as deciding what's important (meaningful) and what isn't. It's a period of trying on a lot of roles to see which ones feel right. Children will at times appear very rambunctious and at other times seem to be only bystanders of people and events. They are *observing everything*.

> **It's a period of trying on a lot of roles to see which ones feel right.**

Implications for Developing Self-Esteem: Here modeling plays an important role. Teachers, parents, and coaches, for example, should be terrific people, worth emulating. This is an open-window stage: Both boys and girls have a similar ability in just about all areas of the curriculum, whether gaining skills in music or soccer. Most all students have a natural curiosity and an almost uncanny ability to achieve in several areas simultaneously. Be sure to provide this student with a variety of opportunities for learning and excelling — regardless of his IQ or his "label."

Ages Thirteen to Fifteen: GO FOR IT! All systems are on GO! here. A child's need to be physical and his curiosity and ability to expand his understanding of the intellectual, social, and spiritual realms are remarkable. Everything is possible, and everything is explored and examined. It's a time of enormous growth in every way; one more stage is being left behind and adolescence is being born.

When viewing the scope of tasks that must be undertaken at this stage, it's no wonder that it's also a time of chaos. Building a solid sense of self and personal worth at this time is probably the toughest and most important task he's ever faced. These are uncharted waters: All learning seems to be a process of trial and error. One of the most difficult is coping with the (physical) growing pains. Physical maturation — internal and external — occurs at an amazing rate. Key hormones are at work now, doing their job of moving this child from preadolescence to full-scale puberty. The awkwardness of physical growth is coupled with the psychic pain of feeling lonely and alone: The fact that boys are about two years behind girls in physical development doesn't help. In fact, the two-year time span in development will even leave some girls out of sync with other girls, causing each one to question why she is (or isn't) growing in this way or that way.

Implications for Developing Self-Esteem: You can best help this age of child maintain high self-esteem through strong support systems during his trials and tribulations, and by not making him feel guilty when his efforts don't work out. You can also help him understand the changes he is going through as well as the pressures he faces, and teach him how to deal with both. The more we give the adolescent a sense of physical and emotional security, the better he will withstand the outside pressures to become what he thinks peers want him to be, and instead, develop along the lines of his interests and talents and aptitudes. In short, he needs adults' friendships.

Age Sixteen: "Excuse Me, But You're in My Way!" This age stands alone because there really is no other age like it. It's not uncommon for this student to experience feelings of being confused, embarrassed, guilty, awkward, inferior, ugly, and scared, all in the same day. In fact, the teenager can swing from childish and petulant behaviors to being sedate, acting rational or irrational all in the same class hour, from intellectual to giddy — back and forth as she tries to figure out just who she is and what's going on with her. It's a time of confusion and uncertainty. Often these swings come complete with easy tears and genuine sobs, high level in-depth sensitivity, great insights and sudden bursts of learning, flare-ups of anger, or boisterous and unfounded giggles. Raging hormones are responsible for ups and downs, as well as for the change in sexual feelings from ambivalent to specific. The goal is to experience intimacy; the self-esteem need is to belong. The task is to learn about oneself as a sexual being (hers, femininity; his, masculinity) and how this is perceived by the opposite sex.

> Feelings of invulnerability and immortality lead youth to behave in reckless ways.

This is a time of duality: She wants to be with others, yet she wants to be alone; she needs her friends, but will sabotage them if they appear to outdo her; she'll root for a friend out loud, but secretly wish for her demise. It's a time when she wants total independence but is by no means capable of it; she doesn't really want to live without her parents, though she believes they are a roadblock stifling her life.

This physical and emotional jumble is hindered by an inability to look ahead and visualize the long-term effects of present behaviors. To tell the student who is skipping class that he might not be admitted to college, or the student who is not studying that he is cheating himself out of an education, is virtually meaningless. Today, this very moment, is what matters. Feelings of invulnerability and immortality lead youth to behave in reckless ways: The "it-can't-happen-to-me" attitude prevails as they drive too fast, have sexual experiences, and experiment with alcohol and drugs. This is truly a time of identity crisis — an age of frustration.

Implications for Developing Self-Esteem: Seek to understand this student's needs as a budding adult rather than a child. Expect a defiance to adult authority. Consider resistance to adults (especially parents and teachers) as part of her need for self-ness, as part of her movement towards independence. She *must* see adults as hopelessly old-fashioned and naive: This helps her complete the act of pulling away and establishes courage for asserting independence — that is, toying with the idea that she can manage life on her own. Most pronounced is her tearing away from her same-sex parent — especially if the bond has been a loving and close one. To emotionally "leave" this loving parent, she'll have to make the parent wrong — how could she possibly want to leave someone wonderful? (Remember, children transfer bonding with parents onto the teacher.)

A great many young people actually do leave home (or threaten to) for three or more days during their sixteenth year. (Ever wonder about that student who mysteriously disappeared for a few days, and then turned up feeling disturbed?) That so many sixteen-year-olds leave home or threaten to is usually done out of frustration and as a way to coerce parents into providing them with more rope to be independent — to gain a bigger share of self-power in making more decisions on their own. The degree of defiance this child has toward parents (and teachers) will depend upon how parental power has been handled in early childhood. This is a good time to help this student learn effective ways to communicate, negotiate, and manage frustration.

Help this student to learn effective ways to communicate, negotiate, and manage frustration.

Ages Seventeen to Eighteen: Establishing Independence. The final stage of development in childhood is establishing total independence (as an individual person, able to assert independence). In looking beyond being dependent on others to dependence on self, this child confronts some big (and frightening) issues. The three tasks are:

1. To determine his vocation: "What am I going to do (for work) with my life?" "Can I afford myself?" Answering these questions gives meaning. Underlying this task is the self-esteem need to be somebody — to experience positive feelings of strength, power, and competence.

2. To establish values: The goal is sort out his *own* values and decide which ones to keep, and which ones to discard. Only in this way can he develop integrity. Perhaps most striking is his need to establish a workable and meaningful philosophy of life. Reevaluating his moral concepts will mean searching for his own personal beliefs, complete with facing religious, ethical and value-laden ideologies. Developing personal convictions will be influenced by his level of self-esteem — especially if there is conflict in what he believes, what he was raised with, and what his friends find acceptable. Will he claim and stay committed to what is true for him? As he ponders the thought, he'll grasp and cling to sweeping idealisms searching for what they must mean as he tries them on for size.

3. To establish self-reliance: Accomplishing this task develops self-trust and confidence. The underlying self-esteem need is to be himself, to look at life through his own lens, and not through the role of student, athlete, son, and so on.

Implications for Developing Self-Esteem: Show respect for this student as an *individual.* Don't expect him to automatically agree with your values. In matters of discussion or disagreement, give him the respect you would give to an adult friend of yours. Ask him for his opinions on adult topics, such as current affairs. Ask him to write about his opinions on moral issues, job decisions, personal problems. Encourage him to think through his own philosophy, to give it more form and substance, to develop and put it into words. He'll need to see that you respect him, that you are helping him learn the process of making decisions, evaluating the consequences, and putting one foot in front of the other in order to go forward into his life.

Encourage him to think through his own philosophy, to give it more form and substance.

Curriculum, Childhood, and Teaching: Programming for Students

Knowing about children's developmental stages is more than just interesting. Used wisely, this information can help you understand children's needs and behaviors, and program into your curriculum the kinds of analogies, stories and examples that best make meaning of the information you want your students to learn. Let's look at what this means for a five-year-old student.

Needing his parents is the "stuff" of the five-year-old. When he's away from the parent, he suffers *separation anxiety*. Now, separation anxiety isn't new; you and I experienced separation anxiety when we were five, and our children's kids are going to have to get over being away from their parents, too. But contemporary times have transformed children's normal fears. Today, five-year-olds worry daily about their parents' *safety*, not just their parents' whereabouts. In other words, normal fears take on new meaning. The five-year-old believes that if his mother or father goes to work (or stays at home during the day), someone will come in the window (the door is still a safety point) and harm the parent. He believes that if the parent uses an elevator at work, someone will come in and "knife" the parent; and if the parent goes into a building that is more than two stories high, just like on *Dallas* (and that's his frame of reference for this fear), there's a good chance of that building getting blown up.

The major insecurity of being without the parent, then, is transformed into a fear of his parents' deaths. The five-year-old wonders whether or not a parent will survive the day in order to pick him up after school or come home at the end of a work day. "My mom is picking me up today," or "My dad is taking me to the zoo this weekend," he assures you. This daydream, or "flashback," occurs three to five times an hour. In this way, the five-year-old student reassures *himself* that his parents are "still okay"; they are safe.

But he's not at his best right now. He's preoccupied, much like you if you are going through a painful separation or divorce, or something else emotionally disturbing. Your mind is preoccupied with sorting it out. Children are emotionally distracted, too. Transferring bonding and trust, accepting others, and learning are at stake for all children. Here's how the five-year-old is affected.

Transferring bonding, and trust, accepting others, and learning are at stake for all children.

■ **The transference of bonding and trust**. When a child comes to school, he transfers parental bonding and trust to the teacher. When you say, "Sit down, let's . . .," the student needs to comply. He must form a trusting relationship with you, the teacher, and that's important because this bond becomes a significant link to his learning. We know that students always transfer onto the teacher the same relationship they have with the same sex parent. When the five-year-old feels secure about his parents, he can more easily transfer positive feelings to his teacher.

■ **Acceptance of others.** Next, the student will need to show acceptance of other students. When he looks around at other students he must conclude, "Gosh, there sure are a lot of kids in here. Rather than hit them, I think I'll talk (and socialize) with them!" We call this view of adjusting to others *socialization* in early childhood, *friendship* when children are older, *popularity* when children get to be teens, and *comradery* in adulthood. In the workforce we use terms like *team players*, *synergy*, and so on. Respect for others begins with acceptance.

Children coping with anxiety do not adjust well to other children. They're generally selfish and rude, and sometimes hostile. They are not liked much by the other students, either. They don't do well in groups, and because they've alienated other students, these children are unkind to them in return. Dealing with such "communication problems" takes up valuable time that could be used for learning.

■ **Learning.** The third task is learning. Since the major issue for the five-year-old is parental anxiety, what does this say about what needs to be in the curriculum? It means that when you read this child a story about other children, he identifies; when you add pets, he's a little more interested; but when you put in a parent and child interacting with one another, you have entered into his emotional security needs. He will be held a captive and curious learner, and his attention span will increase by five to eight minutes. Understanding this student helps you meet his needs while providing for learning to occur. The reading list that you design for your students (and for their parents) should also reflect the needs of your students.

Why Are Children So Different (Fearful) Today?

Why does the five-year-old conjure up images of a parent being hurt or killed while he is away at school? Increased exposure to violence may be one cause. Because television has erased the dividing line between childhood and adulthood programming, children are exposed to everything. The young child who has seen violence on television (or in real life) transposes that image into what he fears could happen to his parents. That's why you *must* ask parents to monitor their child's television viewing. It matters.

I remember, and perhaps you do too, a time when we slowly disclosed to children the contradictions and other personal and social realities of adulthood. We didn't swear in the presence of children and understood why we believed it to be harmful. But today we mostly ignore these common sense practices, probably believing that one way or another children will see and hear it all. We erroneously believe that children don't pay a price for being exposed to violent and hostile messages and images, but they do. Five-year-olds, for example, can't separate reality from fantasy. If a young child imagines a ghost is in his room, the parent doesn't put the ghost under the bed or behind the headboard, right? The parent puts the ghost up in the corner (so to speak) where the child can "see" it, then gives it a friendly name and tells the child that it's there to protect him. The parent creates a fantasy to help the child deal with his fear because he doesn't have the capacity to make it go away. That's why the world of fantasy and imagination is used so often in childhood. It helps children make fears manageable.

How can you dispel those fears so that children can be psychologically comfortable enough to go on to other things, such as being a friend and learner? You do this by knowing and understanding what's going on in and with your students in their developmental stage, and then putting in place those practices designed to provide emotional security — those that allow the child to deal with the fear appropriately. Following through on our five-year-old, here's what you *must* do.

> **We erroneously believe that children don't pay a price for being exposed to violent and hostile messages and images.**

- ■ **Dispel the fear.** If the student you teach is five, the first thing you can do in dispelling the child's fear is to ask that his parents take him to the parents' workplace. It doesn't have to be Monday morning at 8:00; it can be in the afternoon at 4:30, or on a weekend. The goal is to let the child see the parent's workplace as a safe and orderly environment, and to give the child reason to believe that the parent is safe there. Many children have never been to their parents' workplace; most children have no idea what their parents do during the day. The problem with this is that young children may think their parents work with very dangerous people who carry guns and knives, and so on. By visiting the workplace, (young) children can see for themselves that their parents' lives are not in serious danger.

  Older children are frightened when they believe that their parents' well-being is in jeopardy. The *unknown* produces fears for all children. Even the fifteen-year-old is painfully aware of (and often angry about) how much he needs adults. These anxieties keep students from the productive work to be done in childhood, like making and sustaining friends, and of course, learning.

■ **Ask parents to monitor television viewing.** Parents *must* monitor television viewing when their children are young. I advise parents to do so until their children are at least twelve years old. Children pay a very high price for the violence they see on television. Harmful insecurities are created as a result of the impact these images have on young minds.

■ **Talk about parental safety.** Ask parents to talk to their children about their own safety while they are away from their children, and most especially if the parent travels and is away from home often.

The unknown produces fears for all children.

■ **Learn about the "normal" stresses, strains and fears of childhood.** Since many fears are predictable at the various ages and stages of development, you should know what they are. Knowing gives you insight into the motivations of students, and shows you where they need extra support as well as what specific tools they need to manage daily life. In my book, *Stress in Children*, I examine the insecurities at each grade level. Though it's not possible to show all of that research for you here, I'll provide a summary.

Kindergarten:

■ Uncertainty of parental safety

■ Fear of abandonment by parents

■ Fear of punishment/reprimand from teachers, parents, other adults

First Grade:

■ Fear of loud noises, especially that of large trucks and buses

■ Being struck by another student

■ Fear of wetting on themselves in class or in front of others

Second Grade:

■ Fear of not understanding a given lesson (won't be able to spell words for a quiz or pass a test)

■ Not being asked to be a "teacher's helper"

■ Fear of teacher's discipline

Third Grade:

■ Being chosen last on *any* team

■ Fear of not being liked by the teacher

■ Fear of not having enough time to complete schoolwork

■ Being asked to stay after school

Fourth Grade:

- Fear that a friend will betray them, select a different friend, or share "their" secrets
- Fear of ridicule by the teacher or other students
- Fear of not being personally liked by the teacher

Fifth Grade:

- Being chosen first on any team (and being made "an example")
- Fear of losing his or her best friend or that the friend will share "secrets"
- Fear of being unable to complete schoolwork

Children fear ridicule by the teacher or other students.

Sixth Grade:

- Fear of the unknown concerning own sexuality
- Fear of not passing into middle school/junior high
- Fear of peer disapproval of appearance
- Fear of not being liked by another student

Seventh Grade:

- Being selected first (and having to lead) and being picked last (interpreted as being disliked or unpopular)
- Fear of the unknown concerning own sexuality (peers have shared wild stories or myths, compounded by television exposure and popular lyrics)
- Extreme concern and worry about emotional happiness and unhappiness
- Fear of not being able to complete homework/schoolwork/task assignments

Eighth Grade:

- Being selected last (seen as being disliked or unpopular)
- Coming to terms with own sexuality (based on bits and pieces and lack of information concerning sexuality, coupled with inner and outer stages of development)
- Extreme concern and worry about emotional happiness and unhappiness
- Fear of activities that require exposure of the body (physical education)

Ninth Grade:

- Fear of sexuality (too much misinformation from peers)

Older children are concerned over not knowing what to do in life.

- Fear of activities that require exposure of the body (physical education)
- Extreme concern and worry about emotional happiness and unhappiness
- Fear of being challenged to a confrontation by someone of the same sex (getting into a fight)

Tenth Grade:

- Fear of being disliked or unpopular
- Fear that another peer will vie for his or her "sweetheart"
- Fear of not having derived satisfaction from schooling ("I'm not a good student." "I don't do well in school, but I don't know why.")
- Questioning of family harmony in relationships

Eleventh Grade:

- Fear of "not being OK" and ridiculed by class members
- Not having enough money
- Fear that other adults will interpret roles for him (he seeks to try on and define his own values)
- Concern over not knowing what to do in life

Twelfth Grade:

- Fear that other adults will interpret roles for him (he wants to clarify values, goals and relationships for himself)
- Fear of uncertainty — not knowing what to do next year (life outside of school)
- Fear that preoccupation with self-needs (physical, job, career, personal, peer, ego) results in deficiency in school role as a learner ("I just didn't take school seriously." "I don't think I learned anything." "I don't think I'll make it in college.")

Knowing that these stressors create problems for students allows you to talk about them with your students and to help them learn effective ways to deal with them. You should also share these fears with parents. When parents better understand their children's insecurities and help them find workable solutions, students will come to the learning experience less emotionally encumbered. Again, there are many excellent books on children's development, and several are listed in the reference section at the back of this book. You might also want to ask your school district's curriculum director, or director of elementary or secondary education (or your school's counselor or librarian), for additional resources not only to gain knowledge in this area for yourself and to highlight their implications for curriculum development but to assist you in designing parent education programs as well.

Knowing about children is your business. The more you learn about your students, the more capable you are in your role. The more you understand your students, the better able you are to lead students and to instill confidence and inspire them. Educators who feel competent in their work radiate knowledge and educate with confidence.

The more you learn about your students, the more capable you are in your role.

DISCUSSION: A Lesson Plan for Educators

1. How does a "can do" attitude contribute to performance and self-esteem? What can be done to develop a "can do" attitude if it doesn't exist?

2. How does a knowledge of your students and their developmental stages improve your performance as an educator?

3. What fears are common to children and how can an educator help reduce them or lessen their effects on the students? How does a child's fears impact a teacher and that teacher's performance?

Chapter 11

COMPETENCE:
What's Your Philosophy Of Education?

The Role of a Philosophy in Your Teaching

Knowing how to teach is not enough. Content and subject area knowledge is not enough. Inherent in a sense of feeling capable as an educator is knowing not only *what* to teach but *why* to teach it.

At the heart of delineating purposeful activity in teaching is identifying an educational philosophy that helps you to answer value-laden questions and make decisions from among the many choices you have. A philosophy serves to suggest purpose in what you do, and helps you to clarify the objectives and specify the activities that need to be accomplished to reach those goals. A philosophy articulates what *you* want from your teaching. It defines and clarifies your role, and guides the selection of strategies in accomplishing your teaching objectives. Curriculum decisions ultimately reflect differing beliefs and values about what you see as important values to pass on to your students.

A philosophy serves to suggest purpose in what you do.

The benefits of having an educational philosophy are many, as the following list shows. As you read this list, think about the philosophy that guides your actions and enables you to be effective in your role.

- With a philosophy, I can look at ideas about teaching and determine those values that I really want to impart and those I want to change.

- Thinking about what is important to teach guides my actions.

- I become more aware of my strengths — how much I have to offer students, how much I have to share — and this gives me courage and confidence to pull through the tough and challenging times.

- I set goals for myself as an educator and have concrete objectives to work towards. This helps me change what I don't like about my teaching and set new standards.

- I become more clear about what I really want for my students and what I'm actually giving each one.

- I become more aware of my own repressed, but natural, resentments about teaching, such as the lack of freedom and the sacrifices, and am able to acknowledge these in a healthy manner.

The Search for a Philosophical Attitude

Schooling is a moral venture, one that necessitates choosing specific values from among innumerable possibilities. As an educator, you must face and answer some important questions about the purpose of schooling and your role in working with students. For example:

- What is education for?
- What should the school accept responsibility for?
- What kind of citizens and what kind of society do we want?
- What methods of instruction or classroom organization must we provide to produce these desired ends?
- Is the purpose of school to change, adapt to, or accept the social order?
- What educational objectives should be common to all students?
- Should objectives deal with controversial issues, or only those things for which there is established knowledge?
- Should objectives be based on the needs of society in general, or the expressed needs of students?

What kind of citizens and what kind of society do we want?

The Five Educational Philosophies and What They Mean

The five distinct educational philosophies include *perennialism, idealism, realism, experimentalism,* and *existentialism.* Collectively, these philosophies represent a broad spectrum of thought about what schools should be and do. Curriculum experts Wiles and Bondi believe that educators holding differing philosophies would create very different schools for students to attend and learn in. As you read the following descriptions of the five philosophies, try to determine which one most closely matches your own.

- **Perennialism.** The most conservative, traditional, and unchanging of the five philosophies is perennialism. Perennialists believe that students should be taught the world's permanencies through structured study — a curriculum of subjects taught through highly disciplined drill and behavior control. The teacher interprets and tells. The student is a willing recipient.

- **Idealism.** Idealists favor schools teaching subjects of the mind, such as thinking and problem-solving. Teachers serve as models. The function of schools is to sharpen intellectual processes. Students have a somewhat nonparticipatory role, receiving and memorizing the reporting of the teacher.

- **Realism.** This philosophy espouses that the world is as it is, and the job of schools is to teach students about the world. Subjects such as math and science are highly valued. The teacher imparts knowledge. Classrooms are ordered and disciplined.

The experimentalist openly accepts change.

- **Experimentalism.** The experimentalist openly accepts change, for the world is an ever-changing place. The experimentalist favors heavy emphasis on social subjects and experiences. Learning occurs through a problem-solving or inquiry format. Teachers help learners or consult with learners who are actively involved in discovering and experiencing the world in which they live. Group consequences are valued.

- **Existentialism.** For existentialists, the purpose of schools is to assist students in learning about themselves and their place in society. Studies such as the arts, ethics, and philosophy are valued. Teacher-student interaction centers around assisting students in their personal learning journeys.

Telltale Signs: How Others Can Tell What Your Philosophy Is

Classroom space, organization and dissemination of knowledge, uses of learning materials, instructional style, teaching strategies, organization of students, discipline, and student roles are all indicators of your philosophy.

1. **Classroom organization.** A traditional pattern orders the room in such a way that all vision and attention is on the teacher. Activity is "fixed" by the arrangement of furniture so that there is little opportunity for lateral communication. This allows for the teacher lecture-format, but little else. Another possibility is to create multipurpose spaces with the focus of attention generally in the center of the classroom. This style allows for increased student involvement and mobility, and for varied learning activities to take place simultaneously.

2. **Student mobility.** How much movement students are allowed to have in the classroom is another subtle indicator of your philosophy. Movement in some classrooms is totally dependent upon the teacher. Students in such a classroom must request permission to talk, go to the washroom, or approach the teacher. In a less stationary classroom, students move within controlled patterns monitored by the teacher. While the teacher is talking, for instance, movement may not be allowed. At other times, however, students may be able to sharpen pencils, get supplies, or leave the room to go to the restroom or get a drink of water without complete dependence on teacher approval.

3. **Organization of knowledge.** Your philosophy is central to the way you organize and disseminate knowledge. The organization of knowledge can best be understood by viewing it in several dimensions: the pattern of its presentation, the way it is constructed and ordered, its cognitive focus, and the time you take to present it. Most programs of study employ one of three standard curriculum designs: *building blocks design*, *branching design*, or *spiral design*. It is also possible to order knowledge in school programs in terms of *task accomplishment* or simple *teaching processes*.

- **Building blocks design.** This takes a clearly defined body of knowledge and orders it into a pyramid-like arrangement. Students are taught foundational material which leads to more complex and specialized foundational knowledge. Deviations from the prescribed order are not allowed because the end product of the learning design (mastery) is known in advance. The building blocks design is the most structured of curriculum organizations.

- **Branching pattern.** This is a variation of the building blocks design but incorporates limited choice in knowledge to be mastered. The branching design allows for some variability in learning but only within tightly defined boundaries of acceptance.

- **Spiral curriculum.** In this design, knowledge areas are continually visited and revisited at higher levels of complexity. This controls what is taught and learned, and predetermines when the student will receive this knowledge.

- **Task accomplishment.** Knowledge in this program is organized to accomplish specified tasks. The purpose of the learning experience is predetermined, but student interaction with data, in terms of both content and order of content, is flexible. Competency-based skill continuums are examples of this design.

- **Teaching processes.** In this design, knowledge is simply a medium for teaching processes. Reading, for example, can be taught regardless of the particular material used.

4. Uses of learning materials. Your philosophy determines how learning materials are used or not used in your classroom. In some settings, no materials are visible to the observer except, perhaps, textbooks. In other classroom spaces, the volume and variety of learning materials gives the impression of clutter; the room presents a high degree of sensory stimulation.

5. Instructional orientation. Your philosophy greatly influences your instructional style. In some classes, learning is absolutely structured — the teacher controls the flow of data, communication, and assessment, largely through drill. Slightly more flexible is a pattern of didactic teaching whereby the teacher delivers information, controls the exchange of ideas, and enforces the correct conclusions through a question-and-answer session. Still another pattern allows students to experience a learning process and then draw their own conclusions about meaning, thus leaving the learning process open-ended.

6. Teaching strategies. The teaching strategies found in classrooms often provide clues regarding the teacher's philosophy. Such strategies can often be inferred from a teacher's behavior and organizational patterns. For instance, some teachers behave in ways that allow only a single learning interface with students, as in the case of the didactic method. Other teachers provide multiple ways for students to interact and communicate during instruction. Two behaviors that speak louder than words are the *motivational techniques* a teacher uses, and the *interactive distances* between the teacher and student.

> Knowledge areas are continually visited and revisited at higher levels of complexity.

■ **Motivational techniques.** There are a range of motivational techniques. Some techniques seek to control and structure learning while others encourage flexibility.

■ *Threats or fear,* are used by the teacher who seeks maximum structure in the classroom.

■ *Coercion,* as a rule, arrests behavior and encourages conformity to previous patterns of behavior.

■ *Extrinsic rewards,* immediate or deferred, also encourage structure by linking desired behavior with reward.

■ *Intrinsic rewards,* whether immediate or deferred, have the opposite effect. Intrinsic rewards encourage student participation in the reward system and thereby result in a wider range of acceptable behaviors.

Intrinsic rewards encourage student participation in the reward system.

■ **Interactive distance.** Another dimension of the learning strategy in a classroom setting is the interactive distance between the teacher and students. While one educator will walk throughout the classroom, another will teach solely from the head of the room.

7. Organization of students. Your philosophy determines the way you organize your students. You can group students according to age, subject area, room capacity, or by students' needs and interests.

8. Disciplinary measures. Disciplinary techniques used by teachers to influence student behavior are often related to one's philosophy. Some teachers treat all infractions the same regardless of severity. Others may deal only with severe or recurrent discipline problems. There are even those teachers who employ no observable disciplinary measures.

9. Student roles. The roles that students take on in a classroom setting are usually a reflection of what is expected behavior for students. A question that usually receives a telling response for an observer in a classroom is, "How do students learn in this classroom?" The following suggests the range of responses to such a question:

They recite and copy from board.	They listen, take notes, take tests.	They listen, read, question, take tests.	They work on things, read.	They do things that interest them.

Assessing Your Philosophy

Given that your philosophy is so important to your teaching, you should be able to identify it. What is your philosophy? The following self-assessment can help you examine yours.

Philosophy Preference Assessment

© Jon Wiles, Joseph C. Bondi, 1984. Reprinted with permission.

Directions: For each item below, respond according to the strength of your belief, scoring the item on a scale of 1 to 5. A one (1) indicates strong disagreement, a five (5) indicates strong agreement.

1 2 3 4 5   **(1)** Ideal teachers are constant questioners.

1 2 3 4 5   **(2)** Schools exist for societal improvement.

1 2 3 4 5   **(3)** Teaching should center around the inquiry technique.

1 2 3 4 5   **(4)** Demonstration and recitation are essential components of learning.

1 2 3 4 5   **(5)** Students should always be permitted to determine their own rules in the educational process.

1 2 3 4 5   **(6)** Reality is spiritual and rational.

1 2 3 4 5   **(7)** Curriculum should be based on the laws of natural science.

1 2 3 4 5   **(8)** The teacher should be a strong authority figure in the classroom.

1 2 3 4 5   **(9)** The student is a receiver of knowledge.

1 2 3 4 5   **(10)** Ideal teachers interpret knowledge.

1 2 3 4 5   **(11)** Lecture-discussion is the most effective teaching technique.

1 2 3 4 5   **(12)** Institutions should seek avenues toward self-improvement through an orderly process.

1 2 3 4 5   **(13)** Schools are obligated to teach moral truths.

1 2 3 4 5   **(14)** School programs should focus on social problems and issues.

1 2 3 4 5   **(15)** Institutions exist to preserve and strengthen spiritual and social values.

1 2 3 4 5   **(16)** Subjective opinion reveals truth.

1 2 3 4 5   **(17)** Teachers are seen as facilitators of learning.

1 2 3 4 5   **(18)** Schools should be educational "smorgasbords."

1 2 3 4 5   **(19)** Memorization is the key to processing skills.

1 2 3 4 5   **(20)** Reality consists of objects.

1 2 3 4 5   **(21)** Schools exist to foster the intellectual process.

1 2 3 4 5   **(22)** Schools foster an orderly means for change.

1 2 3 4 5   **(23)** There are essential skills everyone must learn.

1 2 3 4 5   **(24)** Teaching by subject area is the most effective approach.

1 2 3 4 5   **(25)** Students should play an active part in program design and evaluation.

1 2 3 4 5   **(26)** A functioning member of society follows rules of conduct.

1 2 3 4 5   **(27)** Reality is rational.

1 2 3 4 5 **(28)** Schools should reflect the society they serve.

1 2 3 4 5 **(29)** The teacher should set an example for the students.

1 2 3 4 5 **(30)** The most effective learning does not take place in a highly structured, strictly disciplined environment.

1 2 3 4 5 **(31)** The curriculum should be based on unchanging spiritual truths.

1 2 3 4 5 **(32)** The most effective learning is nonstructured.

1 2 3 4 5 **(33)** Truth is a constant expressed through ideas.

1 2 3 4 5 **(34)** Drill and factual knowledge are important components of any learning environment.

1 2 3 4 5 **(35)** Societal consensus determines morality.

1 2 3 4 5 **(36)** Knowledge is gained primarily through the senses.

1 2 3 4 5 **(37)** There are essential pieces of knowledge that everyone should know.

Truths are best taught through the inquiry process.

1 2 3 4 5 **(38)** The school exists to facilitate self-awareness.

1 2 3 4 5 **(39)** Change is an ever-present process.

1 2 3 4 5 **(40)** Truths are best taught through the inquiry process.

Philosophy Assessment Scoring

The following sets of questions correspond to each of the five standard philosophies of education:

Perennialist — 6, 8, 10, 13, 15, 31, 34, 37

Idealist — 9, 11, 19, 21, 24, 27, 29, 33

Realist — 4, 7, 12, 20, 22, 23, 26, 28

Experimentalist — 2, 3, 14, 17, 25, 35, 39, 40

Existentialist — 1, 5, 16, 18, 30, 32, 36, 38

Scoring Steps

1. Taking these questions by set (e.g., the eight perennialist questions), record the value of the answer given (i.e., strongly disagree =1). Total the numerical value of each set. In a single set of numbers, the total should fall between 8 (all 1's) and 40 (all 5's).

2. Divide the total score for each set by five (Example 40/5 = 8).

3. Plot the scores.

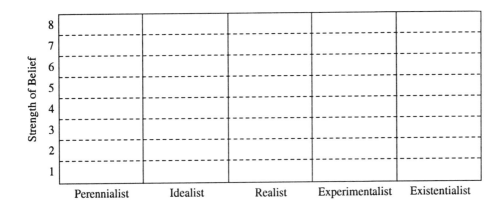

Interpretation

Having plotted your responses on the grid, you now have a profile that gives you an idea of your beliefs about schools. Some patterns are common and therefore subject to interpretation.

Pattern 1. If your profile on the response grid is basically flat, reflecting approximately the same score for each set of questions, it indicates an inability to discriminate in terms of preference.

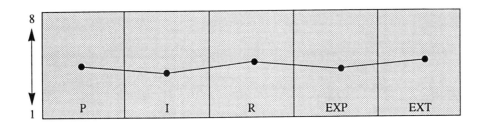

Pattern 2. If your pattern is generally a slanting line across the grid, then you show a strong structured or nonstructured orientation in your reported beliefs.

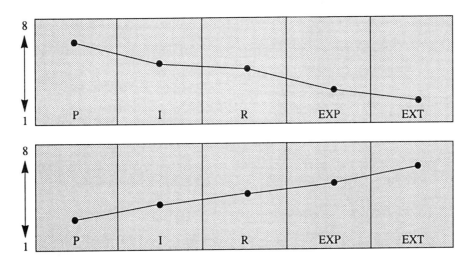

You show a strong structured or nonstructured orientation in your reported beliefs.

Pattern 3. If your pattern appears as a bimodal or trimodal distribution (two or three peaks), it indicates indecisiveness on crucial issues and suggests the need for further clarification. The closer the peaks (adjacent sets), the less contradiction in the responses.

What are the short- and long-term implications of your philosophy?

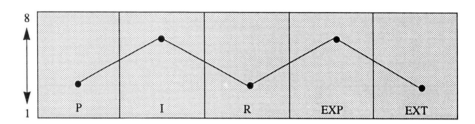

Pattern 4. If the pattern appears U-shaped, a significant amount of value inconsistency is indicated. Such a response would suggest strong beliefs in very different and divergent systems.

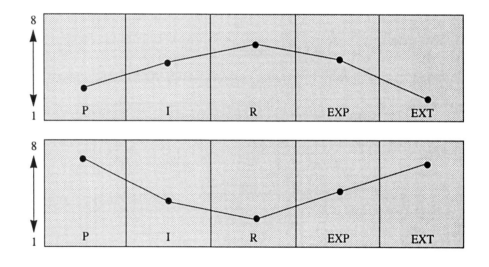

Pattern 5. A pattern which is simply a flowing curve without sharp peaks and valleys may suggest either an eclectic philosophy, or a person only beginning to study his or her own philosophy.

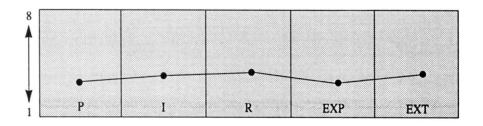

DISCUSSION: A Lesson Plan for Educators

1. Can you articulate your goals, your purpose in becoming an educator? Do you consider that you have met some of your goals and are working toward others? Do you feel you are effective?

2. What is the role of a teaching philosophy? How important is it to be able to articulate one? How did you develop your philosophy? Which of the five basic philosophies (perennialism, idealism, realism, experimentalism, and existentialism) do you support? Is there any benefit to espousing elements of more than one philosophy? Is it possible to do so?

3. How is your teaching philosophy reflected in your daily classroom activities? What are the short- and long-term implications of your philosophy? How can you use your philosophy to motivate students, to improve their performances as well as your own?.

4. How does understanding your philosophy contribute to your effectiveness as an educator?

Chapter 12

MISSION:
Do You Feel Purposeful?

Setting and Achieving Worthwhile Goals

When you have in mind specific goals or intentions of what you want to do and be, you feel vital.

The sixth element of self-esteem is a sense of mission, of feeling purposeful — your life has meaning and direction. When you have in mind specific goals or intentions of what you want to do and be, you feel vital. Because there is vision, there is direction. Going in the direction of what is valuable and purposeful is motivating: You're energized in the process.

An educator who feels purposeful is quite different from one who doesn't. Have you noticed that educators with a sense of purpose seem more vibrant, optimistic, and charismatic, that they have a greater zest and zeal for living than those who do not? Educators who possess a sense of purpose create a contagious excitement that makes them stimulating, invigorating and even attractive.

As Purpose Increases, So Does Performance

When students feel purposeful (or "motivated"), their level of performance goes up. The Coleman Report, a comprehensive investigation of American education, concluded that the degree to which a student felt his life had meaning and direction was the second most significant determinant (parental support was the first) of whether he met with failure or success in his overall effectiveness as a student. This correlation with school success was more important than academic performance, class size, yearly expenditure per pupil, or level of teacher preparation. As a student's sense of purpose increases, so do academic achievement scores; as self-esteem decreases, so does achievement.

A similar connection bears out for adults. A recent Gallup Poll revealed that only 25% of all adults feel purposeful in their work, and even fewer feel an overall satisfaction with their lives!

How did these individuals differ from those who did express satisfaction and a sense of purpose? They said they were working toward two or more goals that were important to them. They also said that they had made a decision to live life in a *zestful* way.

Many of us make the mistake of thinking that a zest for living is a genetic predisposition — that it's something beyond our control — and therefore we don't pursue it. But people who feel that life has purpose have generally designed a personal plan, a growth continuum guided and stimulated by their expectations, whereby success breeds success. Goal-setting leads to goal achievement; satisfaction, pride, and self-esteem lead to an increase in self-confidence, which helps promote an optimistic attitude, resulting in the generation of new goals. Thus, the continuum of goals successfully set and met trigger the cycle of high self-esteem again and again.

Setting goals is an important activity because goals provide direction, signaling where you should focus your time and energy. The first step, of course, is to determine what is of purpose, and then to work toward its accomplishment. Just being busy doesn't necessarily mean your life has focus!

The Nine Key Goals in Life

Below are nine key areas that give meaning and direction to our lives. These areas include peace of mind, quality relationships, learning and education, status and respect, leisure time, health, wellness and fitness, finances, work and career, and other goals that are personally important to us. Read through each of these, then think about the goals you would like to set in each area, and then write out your goals.

Goals
provide
direction,
signaling
where you
should focus
your time
and energy.

- **Goals for Peace of Mind:** The search for meaning and spiritual fulfillment.

_____

_____

_____

_____

- **Relationships:** Goals in relationships (with students, children, colleagues, parents, friends, others).

_____

_____

_____

_____

■ **Learning and Education:** What would you like to know more about?

_____

_____

_____

_____

■ **Status and Respect:** To which groups do you want to belong? From whom do you want respect?

_____

_____

_____

_____

■ **Leisure Time:** What activities (hobbies, sports, travels) would you like to learn more about? To do more of?

_____

_____

_____

_____

■ **Health, Wellness and Fitness:** What are your goals for physical fitness and overall health and wellness?

_____

_____

_____

_____

■ **Financial Goals:** What are your plans for creating enough money to give you the freedom to do the things you want to do?

_____

_____

_____

_____

■ **Productive Work and Career Success:** What are your goals for productive work and career success?

_____

_____

_____

_____

■ **Others:** Which of your goals may not fit into the previous categories, but are important to you?

_____

_____

_____

_____

Guidelines for Setting and Accomplishing Your Goals

A plan for realizing your goals can spell the difference between success and mere wishful thinking. What motivates you to achieve your goals? The following questions can serve as a helpful guide in accomplishing your goals.

■ **Is it _your_ goal?** Have you ever purchased an item of clothing because someone close to you thought it "looked like you" even though you didn't necessarily like it? Chances are, you aren't going to enjoy wearing it as much as if _you_ had a strong desire to own it! Likewise, having a goal that someone else wants you to accomplish — but which is not a priority for

A plan for realizing your goals can spell the difference between success and mere wishful thinking.

you — means you probably won't make the commitment needed to accomplish it! You'll give up when faced with hard work. You need to "own" the goal. This provides the inner fire, a drive that says, "It's important to ME. I will succeed at this."

■ **Is the goal attainable?** Do you believe you can meet your goal? Is it achievable? This doesn't mean that it has to be easy, but there has to be a better than 50-50 chance you can meet the goal. You don't want to set a goal that is self-defeating, one that is so difficult you almost certainly will not achieve it. It's unlikely that you're going to begin and complete a master's degree this year, for example, if you also plan to buy a new home, go to Europe for the summer, and have a baby!

Your goal should also provide a bit of stretch — a challenge. There's a saying that goes, "Most people don't aim too high and miss, they aim too low and hit!" If your goal is to do at least 20 sit-ups and you can already do 19 with no problem, what's the challenge? Build in room to grow.

■ **What makes the goal worth achieving?** What are the benefits? Is it worth the time and effort? When you are lecturing to your students and you say, "Now, this next material will not be on the test, but you should know it anyway," what do your students do? Do they pay as much attention as they normally would, or do they exchange a grin with friends, sit back, and relax? They probably just kick back. They don't take the material seriously because they know they won't be tested on it. They assume there's little benefit to taking notes and paying attention. Can you readily answer the following questions: Why is this goal important to me? How will it contribute/change/expand my life? In what ways does it make me happy? More accomplished? Satisfied? And lastly, what reward have I set for myself at the completion of my goal?

■ **Have you put the goal in writing?** Writing down your goal is important because it helps you clearly identify what you want and increases your personal commitment to it. All of us can cite past instances when our undocumented ideals and goals were unrealized, simply lost in the shuffle of other good intentions. Documenting a goal helps infuse a personal commitment to seeing it through to fruition. It also gives you an opportunity to devise a time-line of the necessary steps to follow in order to realize your goal. Estimate where you are now and where you would like to be, and plan the steps in between.

There's another reason to write down a goal. You internalize or buy into *your* commitment when you put pencil to paper. If it's just in your head, you can easily forget about it. We have thousands of thoughts daily; most are forgotten in moments, but those we take the time and effort to focus on, matter more.

Documenting a goal helps infuse a personal commitment to seeing it through to fruition.

- **Are your goals specific?** Attainable goals are personal decisions and require dedication and commitment. Goals help you stretch and grow and therefore fulfill your potential. Goals that are specific, as opposed to ambiguous, help you clarify the needed direction. For example, rather than saying, "I'd like to be thinner," say, "I'd like to lose 10 pounds over the next 90 days." Commit to writing, as clearly as you can, what you want and what you need to do to realize each of your goals.

- **Are the deadlines realistic?** Goals and deadlines seem a lot easier to reach when they are broken down into manageable tasks. Set dates for each goal, major and minor. Some dates are predetermined — school vacation dates, for example — so you simply have to adjust them to your schedule or to a predetermined calendar. But you can still set intermediate deadlines. Having a date written down helps you to manage the task by prioritizing where and how you will allocate your time. When you see you're nearing a deadline, you can push yourself just a little harder, or know when to plan downtime and playtime. And of course, when you do accomplish a goal within the deadline, you feel successful.

> Goals that are specific, as opposed to ambiguous, help you clarify the needed direction.

- **Have you allowed for periodic self-renewal, for revision and change?** In the growth process of life, it's reasonable to expect that what you want to do and achieve will change and evolve. Consequently, it's a good idea to reevaluate your major goals periodically — at least every six months. This can also promote self-renewal and reduce stagnation. Generating renewed goals helps to revitalize the purpose of your work, the nature of your role, and the direction of your career path. It also serves to nourish objectives and priorities and can even stimulate the formulation of new goals.

- **Have you placed a copy of your goals in sight?** This helps you avoid falling into the "endless activity trap." If you are constantly aware of what your major goal is, you reduce the odds of losing sight of it as you proceed with the whirlwind of daily activities each of us faces. Place a copy on your mirror, in your briefcase, and on the inside of your desk. You might also place a copy on your refrigerator so that family members can know what is of importance to you and allow for the time necessary for you to achieve your plan. When I was completing my first doctorate, I placed a detailed schedule on the refrigerator door where my family could see it. It didn't take long before I heard things like, "Since you have class tonight, I'll cook," or, "Since you have Wednesday off, that might be a good night for us to hit the early movies." Allowing others to zero right in on what is important to us can be very helpful in meeting our goals!

- **When you approach the completion of a major goal, do you begin formulating another goal?** After you achieve one goal and enjoy its rewards, set out in pursuit of the next one. This doesn't mean that you don't take time off, or that you get so goal directed that you don't have time for leisure in your life. A goal may be to take time off from any formalized plans.

Feeling Purposeful: Is Teaching Your Special Calling?

Why did you go into education? Why did you become a teacher? What was the motivation, the attraction? Below are a series of questions to ask yourself. Examine your motives honestly. Don't be harsh on yourself, but be honest. And don't be embarrassed if they are less than altruistic. Not everyone became an educator to change the world, or because they thought it would be rewarding, fulfilling, and just plain fun. Some went into the field for career security, or because they thought it would be the ideal job to have as they raised a family, or because the notion of summers off was appealing to them. Use the following questions to stimulate your thinking.

> **Did you become an educator because an educator encouraged you?**

- Why did you become an educator?
- What prompted you to choose this field?
- Did you respect and admire specific teachers that you had in your youth and want to be like them?
- Did you feel that you had a lot to offer students and wanted to make a difference?
- Did you turn to teaching because it was a secure job at a time when there weren't other opportunities in your field?
- Are your goals the same now as they were then?
- Have you met your goals?
- Has teaching been all you hoped it would be?
- If you were to select a career all over again, would you still choose to be an educator?
- What has been most rewarding about your career?
- Has your career met the idealistic goals you held?
- Do you still feel a sense of purpose when you enter your classroom?
- Do you feel that you are fulfilling a mission?

Who Was Your Favorite Teacher?

Did you become an educator because an educator encouraged you? That's the way most teachers get into the field. Think back to the teachers you had in school — the ones you liked and those you didn't. Name those educators. What did you admire or dislike about them? Use the following questions to stimulate and refresh your memory.

- Who managed to involve you in the subject he or she was teaching and make you *want* to learn?
- Who exuded warmth and compassion?
- Who exuded vitality and excellence?
- Who made you feel that you could ask anything you wanted to about the subject?
- Who made you think and participate in class rather than allow you to hide behind the boy/girl sitting in front of you?
- Who was so exciting that you looked forward to his or her class?
- Who talked *with* students rather than lectured *at* them?
- Who made time fly by because you were busy and involved?
- Who treated all students as part of the class rather than ignored the slow students (because they would require too much work) or the smart ones (because they could take care of themselves)?

Who was so exciting that you looked forward to his or her class?

Did any teacher's name come to mind more than once? Three times or more? If so, you are remembering those teachers who felt their calling, who were genuinely good teachers. Chances are, this is why you became an educator, too.

Can the same be said of you? Are you leaving a similar legacy? Are you an exemplary educator?

DISCUSSION: A Lesson Plan for Educators

1. How important is having a sense of purpose to your teaching performance? How important is having goals in your career? How can you identify what your purpose is in teaching? Do your goals and your purpose change and adapt to reality over the course of your career, or is it important to try to keep those perhaps idealistic goals as long as possible?

2. What are your goals in life, as opposed to those in teaching? What specific goals do you have? How can working toward those goals enhance self-esteem? How can you keep from having your self-esteem lessened when you don't reach a goal or stray far from your original purpose? What makes goals worthwhile and attainable?

3. Why did you become an educator? Would you choose to become a teacher again? What rewards has your career given to you? How has your life been made more fulfilling and fun as an educator than it would have been otherwise? How does viewing yourself as an educator define your life?

AFTERWORD

What Have You Learned by Being an Educator?

"EDUCATION IS THE MOST IMPORTANT PROFESSION, BECAUSE THROUGH THE HANDS OF EDUCATORS, PASS ALL PROFESSIONS."

You discover new strengths within yourself as well.

As you coach your students to discover their potential, you find that you discover new strengths within yourself as well. I know that has been true for me. I've enjoyed many facets of an educational career. Though I am no longer in the classroom, I was a public school educator for a number of years, and served as a director of curriculum at the district level and as an administrator. I've also been a professor at a university, served as the executive director of an educational foundation, and now travel the country as a consultant. My work at all levels has enriched my life. In particular, I've learned the meaning of the following concepts:

■ **Satisfaction.** There is a great deal of satisfaction in seeing a student's face light up as she gets the answer and recognizes that she is indeed capable, able to understand a difficult concept, competent at the task. I feel the satisfaction of knowing that I am helping young people recognize the good in themselves that I see in them every day.

■ **Empathy.** I've had to put myself in my students' places and undergo the frustrations and rewards of learning. This has taught me to be more tolerant and understanding, valuable lessons for the rest of my life, especially as a parent myself.

■ **Patience.** I learned how important this one concept is when seeing how each student learned at a different rate. You can't rush learning — it's experiential. I had to temper my instincts to lead, and let the student set the pace.

■ **Endurance.** This is the one attribute all teachers must have if they are to survive. When dealing with a classroom of 33 youngsters, all different, all important, all worth as much of myself as I could give them, I recognized that I had to be fit and strong. I began a rigorous workout routine that increased my stamina. The side benefits of enhancing my health and wellness were welcomed.

■ **Listening.** Although very young children often say what they mean, older ones let their tones and actions convey the true meaning. I learned, sometimes the hard way, to look beyond just the words in order to understand the feelings behind the message. I became an empathic listener, more intuitive and understanding.

■ **Responsibility.** I quickly learned to rely on myself, as others were counting on me as well. I accepted the responsibility and worked diligently at fulfilling it. This meant understanding my own needs and clarifying my values in order to be at my best. The role of caretaker of young minds is one I take very seriously.

■ **Assertiveness.** As a leader, I must communicate clearly and directly. Children cannot be expected to read between the lines; I learned to make my statements clearly and directly and in sufficient detail. The same is needed in a position of responsibility.

■ **The needs of the students.** I discovered what my students needed from me was not always what I had intended to give. I was forced to expand my horizons, to challenge myself in new ways that were fun and fulfilling.

■ **The nature of adults.** I saw in my students the same types of people that I deal with as adults: clowns, show-offs, prima donnas. The children played their roles much more directly than adults, giving me insights that I might not have had otherwise. Learning to deal with students gave me the knowledge and ability to deal with their adult counterparts.

■ **Self-discipline.** I had to learn to meet deadlines and assume responsibility; people were counting on me, looking up to me as a role model. I learned to take charge of my own life, which no one was going to do for me. I was the adult, the one they depended on. I learned not only to give sound advice, but to take it myself.

■ **The value of self-esteem.** Every day, the classroom was a microcosm, a laboratory that showed me the effects of self-esteem. Those students who felt good about themselves performed above expectations; those students with low self-esteem rarely fulfilled their potential. Daily I saw how students who cared about themselves cared about others; they were more giving, nurturing and responsible. I learned that positive self-regard was central to learning; I also learned that self-esteem was central to teaching.

> The classroom was a microcosm, a laboratory that showed me the effects of self-esteem.

■ **How to be a better person.** I had to be on my best behavior, aware that my students were watching and learning from me. I became a better, wiser, warmer, and more caring person because of them.

■ **How to be a good parent.** From the experience I gained in working with learners, I learned how best to bring about a positive behavioral mind set for my own child. And as I became a better parent, I became a better teacher.

When I became a new parent many years ago, a friend gave me a plaque with this beautiful message. Though written for parents, its time-honored application for educators working with formative minds is unmistakable.

Children Learn What They Live

If a child lives with criticism, he learns to condemn.

If a child lives with hostility, he learns to fight.

If a child lives with ridicule, he learns to be shy.

If a child lives with shame, he learns to feel guilty.

If a child lives with tolerance, he learns to be patient.

If a child lives with encouragement, he learns confidence.

If a child lives with praise, he learns to appreciate.

If a child lives with fairness, he learns justice.

If a child lives with security, he learns to have faith.

If a child lives with approval, he learns to like himself.

If a child lives with acceptance and friendship,

he learns to find love in the world.

I wish you joy and rewards in your work.

Resources and Suggested Readings

Anderson, Eugene; Tedman, George; and Rogers, Charlotte. *Self-Esteem for Tots to Teens*. New York: Meadowbrook/Simon and Schuster, 1984.

Axline, Virginia M. *Dibs: In Search of Self*. New York: Ballantine Books, 1967.

Barksdale, Lilburn S. *Essays on Self-Esteem*. Idyllwild, California: The Barksdale Foundation, 1977.

Beane, James, Lipka, Richard. *Self-Concept, Self-Esteem and the Curriculum*. New York: Teachers College Press, 1984.

Bennett, William. *Schools Without Drugs*. U.S. Department of Education: White House, Washington, D.C. 1989.

Berne, Patricia and Savary, Louis. *Building Self-Esteem in Children*. New York: Continuum, 1989.

Bessell, Ph.D., and Kelly Jr., Thomas P. *The Parent Book*. Rolling Hills Estates, CA: Jalmar Press, 1977.

Bloom, Benjamin and others. *Taxonomy of Educational Objectives: Cognitive and Affective Domains*. NJ: Longman, 1969.

Bloom, Benjamin S. "Affective Outcomes of School Learning." *Phi Delta Kappan* 1977: 193-199.

Borba, Michele. *Esteem Builders*. CA: Jalmar Press, 1989.

Branden, Nathaniel. *Psychology of Self-Esteem*. Los Angeles, CA: Bantam Books, Nash Publishing Co., 1969

Branden, Nathaniel. *What Is Self-Esteem?* First International Conference on Self-Esteem: August 1990, Asker, Norway.

Briggs, Dorothy Corkille. *Celebrate Yourself*. Garden City, New York: Doubleday, 1977

Brookover, W. B. *Self-Concept of Ability and School Achievement*. East Lansing, Mich: Office of Research and Public Info., Michigan State University, 1965.

Buscaglia, Leo. *Living, Loving & Learning*. Thorofare, New Jersey: Charles B. Slack, 1982.

Byer, Barry. *Developing a Thinking Skills Program: Practical Strategies for Teachers*. Allyn Bacon, 1988.

Canfield, Jack, and Wells, Harold C. *100 Ways to Enhance Self-Concept in the Classroom*. Englewood Cliffs, NJ: Prentice-Hall, 1976.

Cetron, Marvin. *Schools of the Future*. New York: McGraw-Hill, 1985.

Chance, Paul. *Thinking in the Classroom: A Summary of Programs*. Teachers College Press. 1986.

Chuska, Kenneth R. *Teaching the Process of Thinking, K—12*. Bloominton, Indiana: Phi Delta Kappa Educational Foundation, 1986.

Combs, A. "Affective Education or None at All." *Educational Leadership,* April 1982.

Coopersmith, Stanley. *The Antecedents of Self-Esteem.* San Francisco, CA: W. H. Freeman, 1967.

Covey, Stephen. *The 7 Habits of Highly Effective People.* New York: Simon and Schuster, 1989.

Covington, M. "Self-Esteem and Failure in School," *The Social Importance of Self-Esteem.* U.C. Press, Berkeley, 1989.

Crockenberg, Susan, and Soby, Barbara. "Self-Esteem and Teenage Pregnancy," *The Social Importance of Self-Esteem.* U.C. Press, Berkeley, CA, 1989.

Dishon, Dee, and O'Leary, Pat Wilson. *A Guidebook for Cooperative Learning: A Technique for Creating More Effective Schools.* Holmes Beach, Florida: Learning Publications, Inc., 1984

Drew, Naomi. *Learning The Skills of Peacemaking.* Rolling Hills Estates, CA: Jalmar Press, 1987.

Earle, Janice. *Female Dropouts: A New Perspective.* Alexandria, VA: National Association of State Boards of Education, 1987.

"Family Fitness: A Complete Exercise Program for Ages Six to Sixty-Plus." *Reader's Digest* (Special Report) 1987, p. 2—12.

Feingold, Norman S., and Miller, Nora Reno. *Emerging Careers: New Occupations for the Year 2000 and Beyond.* Maryland: Garrett Park Press, 1989.

Fensterheim, Herbert. *Don't Say Yes When You Want to Say No.* New York: Dell Publishing Co., 1975.

Fox, Lynn. and Lavin-Weaver, F. *Unlocking Doors to Self-Esteem.* Rollings Hills Estates, CA: Jalmar Press, 1983.

Freed, A. *TA for Tots,* Revised. Rollings Hills Estates, CA: Jalmar Press, 1991.

Freed, A. *TA for Teens.* Rollings Hills Estates, CA: Jalmar Press, 1976.

Freed, A., and Freed, M. *TA for Kids.* Rollings Hills Estates, CA: Jalmar Press, 1977.

Fuellgrabe, U. *Psychological Analysis of Vandalism.* Polizei-Fuehrungsakademie: West Germany, 1980.

Fugitt, Eva D. *He Hit Me Back First!* , Revised, Rolling Hills Estates, California: Jalmar Press, 1983.

Gardner, James E. *Turbulent Teens.* Rolling Hills Estates, CA: Jalmar Press, 1983.

Gibbs, Jeanne. *Tribes: A Process for Social Development and Cooperative Learning.* Center Source Publications: Santa Rosa, CA., 1987.

Ginott, Haim. *Teacher and Child.* New York: Avon, 1972.

Glasser, William. *Schools Without Failure.* New York: Harper & Row, 1969.

Gossop, M. "Drug Dependence and Self-Esteem," *International Journal of Addictions*, Vol II, 1976.

Gribben, Trish. *Pajamas Don't Matter*. Rolling Hills Estates, CA: Jalmar Press, 1979.

Haynes-Klassen. *Learning to Live, Learning to Love*. Rollings Hills Estates, CA: Jalmar Press, 1985.

Holly, William. "Self-Esteem: Does It Contribute to Student's Academic Success?" *Oregon School Study Council*, Univ. of Oregon, 1987.

Holt, John. *How Children Learn*. New York: Delta Books, 1967.

Johnson, David W., and Johnson, Roger T. *Learning Together and Alone: Cooperative, Competitive and Individualistic Learning*, 4th ed. Englewood Cliffs, NJ: Prentice-Hall, Inc., 1987.

Johnston, P. S. "School Failure, School Attitudes and the Self-Concept in Delinquents." *ERIC* Document ED 173—712, 1977.

Kagan, Spencer. *Cooperative Learning Resources for Teachers*. Riverside, CA: School of Education, University of California, 1985.

Kaplan, H. B. *Self-Attitudes and Deviant Behavior*. Goodyear, Pacific Palisades, CA, 1975.

Keegan, Andrew. "Positive Self-Image — A Cornerstone of Success," *Guidepost*. February 19, 1987.

Kehayan, V. Alex. *Partners For Change*. Rolling Hills Estates, CA: Jalmar Press, 1992.

Kehayan, V. Alex. *SAGE: Self-Awareness Growth Experiences*. Rolling Hills Estates, CA: Jalmar Press, 1989.

Kelley, T. M. "Changes in Self-Esteem Among Pre-Delinquent Youths in Voluntary Counseling Relationships." *Juvenile and Family Court Journal*. Vol. 29, May 1978.

Kohlberg, L. and C. Gilligan. "The Adolescent as Philosopher: The Discovery of Self in a Postconventional World." *Daedalus* 100 (4), 1971.

Kreidler, William. *Creative Conflict Resolution: More Than 200 Activities for Keeping Peace in the Classroom*. Glenview, IL: Scott, Foresman and Co., 1984.

Lalli, Judy. *Feelings Alphabet*. Rolling Hills Estates, CA: Jalmar Press, 1984.

Lansky, D, and S. Dorfman, *How To Survive High School with Minimal Brain Damage*. Minneapolis: Meadowbrook, 1989.

Maslow, Abraham. *Toward a Psychology of Being*. New York: D. Van Nostrand, 1962.

McCabe, Margaret E. *The Public High School in the Year 2010: A National Delphi Study*. Dissertation, University of La Verne, La Verne, CA., 1983.

McCabe, Margaret E., and Rhoades, Jacqueline. *How to Say What You Mean*. CA: ITA Publications, 1985.

McDaniel, Sandy, and Bielen, Peggy. *Project Self-Esteem*. Rolling Hills Estates, CA: Jalmar Press, 1990.

McKay, Matthew, and Fanning, Patrick. *Self-Esteem.* Oakland, CA: New Harbinger Publications, 1987.

Montessori, Maria. *The Discovery of the Child.* Notre Dame, Indiana: Fides, 1967.

Moore, Ph.D., Gwen Bailey, and Serby, Todd. *Becoming Whole Through Games* Rolling Hills Estates, CA: Jalmar Press, 1988.

Moorman, Chick, and Dishon, Dee. *Our Classroom: We Can Learn Together.* MI: The Institute for Personal Power, 1983.

Naisbitt, John. *Megatrends.* NJ: Warner Books, 1982.

Newman, Mildred, and Berkowitz, Bernard. *How to Be Your Own Best Friend.* New York: Random House, 1973.

Peale, Norman Vincent. *You Can if You Think You Can.* Pawling, New York: Foundation for Christian Living, 1974.

Postman, N. *The Disappearance of Childhood.* New York: Delacorte Press, 1982.

Raths, Louis E., and others. *Teaching for Thinking: Theories, Strategies, and Activities for the Classroom.* New York: Teachers College Press, 1986.

Reasoner, R., and Gilbert, R. *Building Self-Esteem: Implementation Project Summary.* ERIC Clearinghouse on Counseling and Personnel Services, #CG 020989, 1988.

Samples, Bob. *Metaphoric Mind.* Rollings Hills Estates, CA: Jalmar Press, 1991.

Samples, Bob. *Openmind/Wholemind.* Rollings Hills Estates, CA: Jalmar Press, 1987.

Samson, Richard W. *Thinking Skills: A Guide to Logic and Comprehension.* Stamford, Conneticut: Innovative Sciences, Inc., 1981.

Satir, Virginia. *Peoplemaking.* Palo Alto, California: Science & Behavior Books Inc., 1972.

Scheirer, M. A., and Kraut, R. "Increasing Educational Achievement via Self-Concept Change." *Review of Educational Research,* Winter, 1979.

Schmuck, Richard and Patricia. *A Humanistic Psychology of Education: Making the School Everybody's House.* Palo Alto, CA: Mayfield Publishing Co., 1974.

Schriner, Christan. *Feel Better Now.* Rolling Hills Estates, CA: Jalmar Press, 1990.

Schuller, Robert Charles. *Self-Esteem: The New Reformation.* Waco, Texas: Word Books, Inc., 1982.

Sexton, Thomas G., and Poling, Donald, R. *Can Intelligence Be Taught?* Bloomingdale, Indiana: Phi Delta Kappa Educational Foundation, 1973.

Sheehy, Gail. *Pathfinders,* New York: Morrow, 1981.

Sheinkin, D. Food, *Mind and Mood.* New York: Warner Books, 1980.

Shles, L. *Aliens in My Nest.* Rollings Hills Estates, CA: Jalmar Press, 1988.

Shles, L. *Moths & Mothers/Feathers & Fathers.* Rollings Hills Estates, CA: Jalmar Press, 1989.

Shles, L. *Do I Have to Go to School Today?* Rollings Hills Estates, CA: Jalmar Press, 1989.

Shles, L. *Hugs & Shrugs.* Rollings Hills Estates, CA.: Jalmar Press, 1987.

Shles, L. *Hoots & Toots & Hairy Brutes?* Rollings Hills Estates, CA: Jalmar Press, 1989.

Simpson, Bert K., Ph.D. *Becoming Aware of Values.* La Mesa, California: Pennant Press, 1973.

Skoguland, Elizabeth R. *To Anger With Love.* New York: Harper & Row, 1977.

Smith, Manuel J. *When I Say No I Feel Guilty.* New York: Bantam, 1975.

Sparks, Asa H. *Two Minute Lover.* Rolling Hills Estates, CA: Jalmar Press, 1989.

Steffenhagen, R. A., & Burns, Jeff D. *The Social Dynamics of Self-Esteem.* New York, NY: Praeger, 1987.

Steiner, C. *Original Warm Fuzzy Tale.* Rollings Hills Estates, CA: Jalmar Press, 1977.

Ungerleider, D. *Reading, Writing and Rage.* Rollings Hills Estates, CA: Jalmar Press, 1985.

Vennard, Jane. *Synergy.* Novato, California: Academic Therapy Publications, 1978.

Viscott, David *The Language of Feelings.* New York: Pocket Books, 1976.

Vitale, Barbara M. *Unicorns Are Real.* Rollings Hills Estates, CA: Jalmar Press, 1982.

Vitale, Barbara M. *Free Flight.* Rollings Hills Estates, CA: Jalmar Press, 1986.

Waas, Ph.D., Lane Longino. *Imagine That!* Rolling Hills Estates, CA: Jalmar Press, 1991.

Winn, Marie. *Children Without Childhood.* New York: Pantheon Books, 1981.

Worsham, Antoinette M. and Stockton, Antoinette M. and Stockton, Anita J. *A Model for Teaching Thinking Skills: The Inclusion Process.* Bloomingdale, Indiana: Phi Delta Kappa Educational Foundation, 1986.

Wright, E. *Good Morning Class —I Love You!* Rollings Hills Estates, CA: Jalmar Press, 1989.

Young, Elaine. *I Am A Blade Of Grass.* Rolling Hills Estates, CA: Jalmar Press, 1989.

Youngs, Bettie B. *Stress in Children: How to Recognize, Avoid and Overcome It.* New York: Avon, 1985.

Youngs, Bettie B. *Is Your Net-Working? A Complete Guide to Building Contacts and Career Visibility.* New York: John Wiley & Sons, 1989.

Youngs, Bettie B. *Friendship Is Forever, Isn't It?* Rolling Hills Estates, CA: Jalmar Press, 1990.

Youngs, Bettie B. *The 6 Vital Ingredients of Self-Esteem and How to Develop Them in Your Child.* New York: Macmillan, 1992.

Youngs, Bettie B. *The 6 Vital Ingredients of Self-Esteem and How to Develop Them in Your Students.* Rolling Hills Estates, CA: Jalmar Press, 1992.

Youngs, Bettie B. *Goal Setting Skills for Young People.* Rolling Hills Estates, CA: Jalmar Press, second edition, 1992 .

Youngs, Bettie B. *Stress Management Guide for Educators.* Rolling Hills Estates, CA: Jalmar Press, 1992.

Youngs, Bettie B. *You and Self-Esteem: It's The Key to Happiness & Success*. Rolling Hills Estates, CA: Jalmar Press, 1992.

Youngs, Bettie B. *A Stress -Management Guide for Administrators*. Rolling Hills Estates, CA: Jalmar Press, 1993.

Youngs, Bettie B. *A Stress Management Guide for Young People*. Rolling Hills Estates, CA: Jalmar Press, second edition, 1993.

Youngs, Bettie B. *Problem Solving Skills for Children*. Rolling Hills Estates, CA: Jalmar Press, second edition, 1993.

Youngs, Bettie B. *The Teenager: A Guide to the Adolescent Years*. Deerfield Beach, FL: Health Communications, 1993.

Help Organizations

Many organizations, some with toll-free 800 phone numbers, provide helpful information, among them:

Alcoholics Anonymous
World Services, Inc.
468 Park Ave. South
New York, NY 10016
(212) 686-1100

Al-Ateen, Al-Anon Family Group Headquarters
P.O. Box 182
New York, NY 10159-0182

Alcoholics Anonymous is an international fellowship of men and women who share the common problem of alcoholism. Family members of alcoholics can receive help through groups associated with Alcoholics Anonymous, mainly Al-Anon and Al-Ateen. Al-Ateen chapters are listed in some phone books or you can contact a local Al-Anon group for more information.

Big Brothers/Big Sisters of America
230 North Thirteenth St.
Philadelphia, PA 19107
(215) 567-7000

Big Brothers/Big Sisters of America is a national youth-serving organization based on the concept of a one-to-one relationship between an adult volunteer and an at-risk child, usually from a one-parent family. With more than 495 agencies located nationwide, the organization is dedicated to providing children and youth with adult role models and mentors who help enrich the children's lives, as well as their own, through weekly interaction. Volunteers go through a screening process before being accepted into the program, and professional caseworkers provide assistance, support, and on-going supervision for all matches. Check the white pages of your phone book for the agency nearest you.

Boys' National Hotline
(800) 448-3000 (toll-free)
This hotline provides emergency crisis counseling.

Family Service America (FSA)
11700 West Lake Park Drive
Park Place
Milwaukee, WI 53224
(414) 359-1040

FSA is a membership organization of agencies that deals with family problems serving more than 1000 communities throughout the United States and Canada. Member agencies serve families and individuals through counseling, advocacy, and family life education. Consult the phone book for the agency nearest you.

National Center for Missing and Exploited Children
2101 Wilson Blvd., Ste. 550
Arlington, VA 22021
(703) 235-3900

The center assists families, citizens' groups, law enforcement agencies, and governmental institutions. The center also has a toll-free number for reporting information that could lead to the location and recovery of a missing child. The number is (800) 843-5678.

National Child Abuse Hotline
P.O. Box 630
Hollywood, CA 90028
(800) 422-4453 (toll-free)

The National Child Abuse Hotline handles crises calls and information and offers referrals to every county in the United States. The hotline is manned by professionals holding a master's degree or Ph.D. in psychology. The hotline also provides literature about child abuse prevention. This program is sponsored by Childhelp USA, which is located in Woodland, CA.

National Clearinghouse for Alcohol and Drug Information (NCADI)
P.O. Box 2345
Rockville, MD 20852
(301) 468-2600
(800) 729-6686 (toll-free)

NCADI is the information component of the Office for Substance Abuse Prevention (OSAP) of the U.S. Dept. of Health and Human Services. The clearinghouse maintains an inventory of hundreds of publications developed by Federal agencies and private sector organizations. Most publications are free or are available in bulk quantities for a small fee. NCADI also offers fact verification, video loans, and dissemination of grant announcements and application kits. NCADI provides access to the Prevention Materials Database, an online computer database designed to help select specific items from the NCADI's collection of prevention materials. NCADI publishes "Prevention Pipeline," a bimonthly publication that contains the latest information about research, resources, and activities within the prevention field.

National Council for Self-Esteem
P.O. Box 277877
Sacramento, CA 95827-7877
(916) 455-NCSE
(916) 454-2000

The NCSE is dedicated to promoting and developing quality self-esteem information. The NCSE's mission is to spread the ethics of self-esteem throughout the United States. The organization seeks to ensure that self-esteem information is readily available to those who seek it. Operating as Self-Esteem Central, the NSCE collects information on the best self-esteem curriculums, school programs, drug prevention programs, drop-out prevention programs, study courses, videos, and audio tape programs. Self-Esteem Central houses the National Self-Esteem Library, reported to be the largest collection of self-esteem resources in the world. The library offers research assistance and audio tape programs. The "Self-Esteem Today" newsletter offers the latest in new ideas to develop self-esteem, including current research, model programs, and upcoming conference information. More than 50 local Self-Esteem Councils exist in 20 states. For more information, or to start a council in your city, write the NSCE.

National Institute on Drug Abuse
P.O. Box 100
Summit, NJ 07901
(800) COCAINE (toll-free)

The National Institute on Drug Abuse hotline is a confidential drug abuse treatment referral service. The hotline provides information on local referrals and help for drug abusers and other concerned individuals.

National Runaway Switch Board
(800) 621-4000 (toll-free)

National Youth Work Alliance
1346 Connecticut Ave, N.W.
Washington, D.C. 20036
Offers local referrals for runaway or teen crisis shelters.

Parents Anonymous (P.A.)
7120 Franklin
Los Angeles, CA 90046
(800) 421-0353 (toll-free, outside CA)
(800) 352-0386 (toll-free, CA)

P.A. is a self-help program for parents under stress and for abused children. There are no fees and no one is required to reveal his or her name. Group members support and encourage each other in searching out positive alternatives to the abusive behavior in their lives. To locate a P.A. in your area, call the toll-free hotline numbers listed above.

Crisis counseling and information available 24 hours a day, seven days a week.

Stepfamily Association of America, Inc.
215 Centennial Mall South, Suite 212
Lincoln, NE 68508
(402) 477-STEP

Stepfamily Association of America provides education, information, support, and advocacy for stepfamilies. Publications include a quarterly newsletter, *Stepfamilies*, and the book, *Stepfamilies Stepping Ahead*. Local chapters offer classes, workshops, and support groups for stepfamilies. Members of SAA may attend these meetings at no charge.

Suicide Prevention

Almost every state and major city has one or more suicide hotlines and/or suicide prevention centers. For centers in your area, check with your phone operator, or the State, City, or County Health & Human Services headings in your phone book.

United Way, Inc.

Check the phone book to contact the United Way organization in your area to find the Family Services Agency nearest you. These organizations offer a variety of family counseling services.

DISCOVER materials for positive self-esteem.
CREATE a positive environment in your classroom or home by opening a world of understanding.

Good Morning Class - I Love You (Staff)

Contains thought provoking quotes and questions about *teaching from the heart*. Helps love become an integral part of the learning that goes on in every classroom. Great for new teachers and for experienced teachers who sometimes become frustrated by the system. Use this book to begin and end your day. Greet your students every day with: *"Good morning class - I love you."*

Esther Wright, M.A.

0-915190-58-3, 80 pages, **JP-9058-3 $7.95**
5½ x 8½, paperback, illus./**Button $1.50**

Enhancing Educator's Self-Esteem: It's Criteria #1 (Staff)

For the educator, a *healthy self-esteem* is job criterion No. 1! When high, it empowers us and adds to the vitality of our lives; when low it saps energy, erodes our confidence, lowers productivity and blocks our initiative to care about self and others. Follow the *plan of action* in this great resource to develop your self-esteem.

0-915190-79-6, 144 pages, **JP-9079-6 $16.95**
8½ x 11, paperback

NEW

Bettie B. Youngs, Ph.D.

NOT JUST AUTHORS BUT RESEARCHERS AND PRACTITIONERS.

I Am a Blade of Grass (Staff)

Create a school where all — students, teachers, administrators, and parents — see themselves as both learners and leaders *in partnership*. *Develop* a new *compact for learning* that focuses on results, that promotes *local initiative* and that *empowers* people at all levels of the system. How to in this *collaborative curriculum*. Great for self-esteem.

Elaine Young, M.A. with R. Frelow, Ph.D.

0-915190-54-0, 176 pages, **JP-9054-0 $14.95**
6 x 9, paperback, illustrations

Stress Management for Educators: A Guide to Manage Our Response to Stress (Staff)

Answers these significant questions for educators: *What is stress?* What causes it? How do I cope with it? What can be done to manage stress to moderate its negative effects? Can stress be used to advantage? How *can educators be stress-proofed* to help them remain at *peak performance?* How do I keep going in spite of it?

0-915190-77-X, 112 pages, **JP-9077-X $12.95**
8½ x 11, paperback, illus., charts

NEW

Bettie B. Youngs, Ph.D.

NOT JUST WRITTEN BUT PROVEN EFFECTIVE.

He Hit Me Back First: Self-Esteem Through Self-Discipline (Gr. K-8)

By whose authority does a child choose right from wrong? Here are *activities* directed toward *developing* within the child an *awareness* of his own *inner authority* and ability to choose (will power) and the resulting sense of *responsibility*, freedom and *self-esteem*. 29 seperate activities.

Eva D. Fugitt, M.A.

0-915190-64-8, 120 pages, **JP-9064-8 $12.95**
8½ x 11, paperback, appendix, biblio.

Let's Get Together! (Gr. K-6)

Making friends is easy with the activities in this thoroughly researched book. Students are paired, get to know about each other, produce a book about their new *friend*, and present it in class. Exciting activities help discover commonalities. Great *self-esteem booster*. Revised after 10 years of field testing. Over 150 activities in 18 lessons.

0-915190-75-3, 192 pages, **JP-9075-3 $19.95**
8½ x 11, paperback, illustrations, activities

NEW

C. Lynn Fox, Ph.D.

100% TESTED — 100% PRACTICAL — 100% GUARANTEED.

Feel Better Now: 30 Ways to Handle Frustration in Three Minutes or Less (Staff/Personal)

Teaches people to *handle stress as it happens* rapidly and directly. This basic requirement for *emotional survival* and *physical health* can be learned with the methods in this book. Find your own recipe for relief. Foreword: Ken Keyes, Jr. *"A mine of practical help"* — says Rev. Robert Schuller.

Chris Schriner, Rel.D.

0-915190-66-4, 180 pages, **JP-9066-4 $9.95**
6 x 9, paperback, appendix, bibliography

Peace in 100 Languages: A One-Word Multilingual Dictionary (Staff/Personal)

A candidate for the Guinness Book of World Records, it is the *largest/smallest dictionary ever published*. Envisioned, researched and developed by *Russian peace activists*. Ancient, national, local and special languages covered. A portion of purchase price will be donated to joint U.S./Russian peace project. **Peace Button $1.50**

0-915190-74-5, 48 pages, **JP-9074-5 $9.95**
5 x 10, glossy paperback, full color

NEW

By:
M. Kabattchenko,
V. Kochurov,
L. Koshanova,
E. Kononenko,
D. Kuznetsov,
A. Lapitsky,
V. Monakov,
L. Stoupin, and
A. Zagorsky

ORDER NOW FOR 10% DISCOUNT ON 3 OR MORE TITLES.

NEW

The Learning Revolution
How to learn anything five times faster, better, easier

The Learning Revolution (Adult)

A revolution is changing your life and your world. Here's a book that tells how this revolution is taking shape in America and how it can give us the world's best educational system by the year 2000. That revolution is gathering speed -- a revolution that can help us learn anything five times faster, better, and easier. A must reading for parents, teachers and business people.

Gordon Dryden, Jeannette Vos, Ed.D.

1-880396-24-6, 512 pages, **JP9624-6 $24.95**
6 x 9, paperback, many quotes

Reading, Writing and Rage (Staff)

An autopsy of one profound *school failure*, disclosing the complex processes behind it and the *secret rage* that grew out of it. Developed from educational therapist's viewpoint. A must reading for anyone working with the *learning disabled*, *functional illiterates* or *juvenile delinquents*. Reads like fiction. Foreword by Bruce Jenner.

0-915190-42-7, 240 pages, **JP-9042-7 $16.95**
5½ x 8½, paperback, biblio., resources

D. Ungerleider, M.A.

ORDER FROM: B.L. Winch & Associates/Jalmar Press, Skypark Business Center, 2675 Skypark Drive, Suite 204, Torrance, CA 90505
CALL TOLL FREE — (800) 662-9662 • (310) 784-0016 • FAX (310) 784-1379 • Add 10% shipping; $3 minimum   5/93

DISCOVER books on self-esteem for kids.
ENJOY great reading with Warm Fuzzies and Squib, the adventurous owl.

Larry Shles, M.A.

Moths & Mothers/Feathers & Fathers: The Story of Squib, The Owl, Begins (Ages 5-105)

Heartwarming story of a tiny owl who cannot fly or hoot as he learns to put words with his feelings. He faces frustration, grief, fear, guilt and loneliness in his life, just as we do. Struggling with these *feelings*, he searches, at least, for *understanding*. *Delightfully illustrated.* Ageless.

0-915190-57-5, 72 pages, **JP-9057-5 $7.95**
8½ x 11, paperback, illustrations

Hoots & Toots & Hairy Brutes: The Continuing Adventures of Squib, The Owl (Ages 5-105)

Squib, who can only toot, sets out to learn how to give a mighty hoot. Even the *owl-odontist* can't help and he fails completely. Every reader who has struggled with *life's limitations* will recognize his own *struggles* and *triumphs* in the microcosm of Squib's forest world. A parable for all ages.

0-915190-56-7, 72 pages, **JP-9056-7 $7.95**
8½ x 11, paperback, illustrations

Larry Shles, M.A.

NOT JUST AUTHORS BUT RESEARCHERS AND PRACTITIONERS.

Larry Shles, M.A.

Hugs & Shrugs: The Continuing Saga of Squib, The Owl (Ages 5-105)

Squib feels *lonely, depressed* and *incomplete.* His reflection in the pond shows that he has lost a piece of himself. He thinks his missing piece fell out and he searches in vain outside of himself to find it. Only when he discovers that it fell in and not out does he *find inner-peace* and *become whole.* Delightfully illustrated. Ageless.

0-915190-47-8, 72 pages, **JP-9047-8 $7.95**
8½ x 11, paperback, illustrations

Aliens in my Nest: Squib Meets the Teen Creature (Ages 5-105)

What does it feel like to face a snarly, surly, defiant and non-communicative older brother turned *adolescent*? Friends, dress code, temperament, entertainment, room decor, eating habits, authority, music, isolation, *internal and external conflict* and many other *areas of change* are *dealt with.* Explores how to handle every situation.

0-915190-49-4, 80 pages, **JP-9049-4 $7.95**
8½ x 11, paperback, illustrations

Larry Shles, M.A.

NOT JUST WRITTEN BUT PROVEN EFFECTIVE.

DO I HAVE TO GO TO SCHOOL TODAY?
SQUIB MEASURES UP!

Larry Shles, M.A.

Do I Have to Go to School Today? Squib Measures Up! (Ages 5-105)

Squib *dreads* going to *school.* He day-dreams about all the reasons he has not to go: the school bus will swallow him, the older kids will be mean to him, numbers and letters confuse him, he is too small for sports, etc. But, in the end, he *goes because* his *teacher accepts him "just as he is."* Very esteeming. Great metaphor for all ages.

0-915190-62-1, 64 pages, **JP-9062-1 $7.95**
8½ x 11, paperback, illustrations

**Scooter's Tail of Terror
A Fable of Addiction and Hope (Ages 5-105)**

Well-known author and illustrator, Larry Shles, introduces a new forest character — a squirrel named Scooter. He faces the challenge of addiction, but is offered a way to overcome it. As with the Squib books, the story is *simple*, yet the message is *dramatic.* The story touches the child within each reader and *presents the realities of addiction.*

0-915190-89-3, 80 pages, **JP-9089-3 $9.95**
8½ x 11, paperback, illustrations

NEW

SCOOTER'S TAIL OF TERROR
A TAIL OF ADDICTION AND HOPE

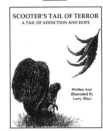

Written And Illustrated By Larry Shles

Larry Shles, M.A.

100% TESTED — 100% PRACTICAL — 100% GUARANTEED.

REVISED

Alvyn Freed, Ph.D.

TA for Tots (and other prinzes) Revised (Gr. PreK-3)

Over 500,000 sold. New upright format. Book has helped thousands of young *children* and their *parents* to better *understand* and *relate to each other.* Helps youngsters realize their *intrinsic worth* as human beings; builds and strengthens their *self-esteem. Simple* to understand.
Coloring Book $1.95 / I'm OK Poster $3

0-915190-73-7, 144 pages, **JP-9073-7 $14.95**
8½ x 11, paperback, delightful illustrations

TA for Kids (and grown-ups too) (Gr. 4-9)

Over 250,000 sold. An ideal book to help youngsters *develop self-esteem,* esteem of others, *personal and social responsibility,* critical thinking and independent judgment. Book recognizes that each person is a unique human being with the capacity to learn, grow and develop. Hurray for TA! Great for parents and other care givers.

0-915190-09-5, 112 pages, **JP-9009-5 $9.95**
8½ x 11, paperback, illustrations

Alvyn Freed, Ph.D.
& Margaret Freed

ORDER NOW FOR 10% DISCOUNT ON 3 OR MORE TITLES.

T.A. FOR TEENS
ALVYN M. FREED PhD

Alvyn Freed, Ph.D.

TA for Teens (and other important people) (Gr. 8-12)

Over 100,000 sold. The book that tells teenagers they're OK! Provides help in growing into adulthood in a mixed-up world. Contrasts freedom and irresponsibility with knowing that *youth need* the *skill, determination* and *inner strength* to reach *fulfillment* and *self-esteem.* No talking down to kids, here.

0-915190-03-6, 258 pages, **JP-9003-6 $21.95**
8½ x 11, paperback, illustrations

The Original Warm Fuzzy Tale (Gr. Pre K-Adult)

Over 100,000 sold. The concept of Warm Fuzzies and Cold Pricklies originated in this delightful story. A *fairy tale* in every sense, *with* adventure, fantasy, heroes, villians and a *moral.* Children (and adults, too) will enjoy this beautifully illustrated book. **Songs of Warm Fuzzy Cass. $12.95. Warm Fuzzies, JP-9042 $0.99 each.**

0-915190-08-7, 48 pages, **JP-9008-7 $8.95**
6 x 9, paperback, full color illustrations

The Original
WARM FUZZY TALE

Claude Steiner, Ph.D

ORDER FROM: B.L. Winch & Associates/Jalmar Press, Skypark Business Center, 2675 Skypark Drive, Suite 204 , Torrance, CA 90505
CALL TOLL FREE — (800) 662-9662 • (310) 784-0016 • FAX (310) 784-1379 • Add 10% shipping; $3 minimum

5/93

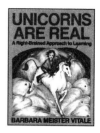

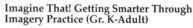

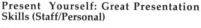